Please Take a Number

To Marci

Let _NUMBERS_ lead you

to SUCCESS!

Vikki MacKinnon

Please Take a Number

Numerology for Real Life
and Everyday Success

Vikki MacKinnon

BALBOA.
PRESS
A DIVISION OF HAY HOUSE

Balboa Press books may be ordered through booksellers or by contacting:

Balboa Press
A Division of Hay House
1663 Liberty Drive
Bloomington, IN 47403
www.balboapress.com
1-(877) 407-4847

Because of the dynamic nature of the Internet, any web addresses or links contained in this book may have changed since publication and may no longer be valid. The views expressed in this work are solely those of the author and do not necessarily reflect the views of the publisher, and the publisher hereby disclaims any responsibility for them.

The author of this book does not dispense medical advice or prescribe the use of any technique as a form of treatment for physical, emotional, or medical problems without the advice of a physician, either directly or indirectly. The intent of the author is only to offer information of a general nature to help you in your quest for emotional and spiritual well-being. In the event you use any of the information in this book for yourself, which is your constitutional right, the author and the publisher assume no responsibility for your actions.

Any people depicted in stock imagery provided by Thinkstock are models, and such images are being used for illustrative purposes only.
Certain stock imagery © Thinkstock.

ISBN: 978-1-4525-4901-9 (sc)
ISBN: 978-1-4525-4902-6 (hc)
ISBN: 978-1-4525-4900-2 (e)

Library of Congress Control Number: 2012904868

Printed in the United States of America

Balboa Press rev. date: 7/9/2012

Dedication

To Garry, Stuart, and Caitlin, who continue to fill my days with love and laughter.

Acknowledgements

It is with deepest gratitude that I acknowledge the following people who have played such an important part in the writing of this book and in my ongoing work:

My editor, Wendy Zak, for her timely support and constructive feedback;

My clients and students who have shared their life stories with me—it is a privilege to serve you;

My parents Gordon Bell and the late Gelda Bell, who instilled in me a love of learning and a desire to serve;

My husband and personal "computer wizard", David MacKinnon, whose love and ongoing support has made it possible to complete this and many other projects.

Contents

Preface

This is a book about you—your days, your months, your years—your life.

This is a book about time—your time, and an amazingly accurate and effective system for making the best possible use of it.

This is a book about energy—the energy of numbers and how they affect you every day and in every way through temporary vibrations.

Numerology has been my passion for thirty years, and my full time career since 2002. I have done readings for clients in North America, Britain, Asia, and the Middle East, and facilitated workshops in Canada and Japan. I am constantly receiving cards and e-mails from students and clients who share with me that working consciously with the energy of their personal numbers has empowered them to:

- ○ Ease stressful situations

- ○ Create more harmony in their relationships

- ○ Restore confidence in themselves

- ○ Overcome financial problems

- ○ Gain clarity and a greater sense of direction

- ○ Turn lessons into blessings, and

- ○ Make the most of new opportunities

Nothing is more important than your Peace of Mind. Nothing is more important than knowing that your life is functioning well, that your key relationships are on solid ground, that you have accepted disappointments and gained strength from adversity, and that you are meeting your responsibilities while competently moving forward in the direction of your dreams.

As you read Please take a Number and connect with the energy of your personal temporary numbers you will learn strategies for dealing with situations or relationships that compromise your Peace of Mind.

Connecting, and working consciously with the energy of your temporary vibrations will erase doubt and bring you to a place of certainty that you are making the right choices and that "the Universe is unfolding as it should".

While all parts of your numerology profile offer guidance, validation, and profound insight, it is very often the temporary vibrations that shed the most light on your immediate circumstances, and reveal the path of least resistance.

In Please Take a Number you will learn how the energy of numbers changes from day to day, month to month, and year to year. More importantly, you will learn a simple and reliable system for using this ever changing energy in positive and pro-active ways; so that you too can achieve the same results that my clients and students have achieved in working with their numbers.

Your Personal Number System is an accurate and reliable tool for proactive living. It is easy to learn and easy to integrate into your lifestyle; and it will help you to gain greater satisfaction in all areas of your life. Whether you are handling day to day responsibilities, working on a short term project, planning a vacation, or making a major life altering decision, you will be amazed at how well your plans come together and how successful you feel when you live in harmony with the energy of your own personal temporary number vibrations.

It has been richly rewarding to share this system in my workshops and private sessions. Now it brings me great pleasure to share it with you.

Introduction

My Journey with Numbers

For the past thirty years, since my journey with numbers began, I have always known the number of my personal year, and how to work with it in making major decisions about my life. I have known the number of my personal month, and understood how to work with that energy in planning certain short term projects.

Every day for that entire period of time, I have known the number of my personal day, and how that number is affecting the day's activities and interactions. Over the years I have learned what types of activities work best within the context of these temporary vibrations, what to avoid, and how to use the energy of each number to its greatest advantage.

Whenever it has been within my power to do so, I have planned my personal and professional commitments to make the most of my temporary numbers. Numerology has been my system for proactive living.

I have also been aware of the numbers that are influencing my husband and family members, and have made every effort to blend the energy of our personal days, months, and years for maximum benefit.

At the age of thirty-seven, I became a single mother. That year, my children were thirteen, six, and one and a half years old. In addition to my responsibilities as a mother, I had a demanding career as an elementary school teacher. My workload was staggering!

I read about time management and incorporated some positive and helpful techniques into my life, but it seemed that the material I was reading had been prepared for men with rising careers in the corporate sector. It was hard for me, as an exhausted and overworked school teacher and single mother of three, to relate to most of the principles and strategies that were set out in this material.

Knowing my personal day, month, and year was infinitely more helpful than trying to follow a system designed for business leaders. It not only gave me an opportunity to work consciously with the energy of numbers, but it also helped me to accept the more challenging times, knowing that tomorrow, next month, and next year, would bring a different kind of energy and experience. I knew that no matter how it seemed to me, there was a logical progression, and it was all unfolding in Perfect and Divine Order.

Part One
Understand the Basics

What Is Numerology and What Can It Do For You?

Numbers are centres of energy—great cosmic forces that lead us to our highest level of integrity and personal fulfillment. They represent areas of learning and stages in our growth. Each of the numbers 1 to 9, and the master numbers 11, 22, and 33, carries a variety of elements and qualities that can be expressed in positive and negative ways, depending on the development and spiritual/ethical maturity of the individual.

Numerology is an ancient science based on the measurement of energy through numbers. Every letter in your name represents numeric energy that affects the qualities you develop and refine in this life time, and the inner strengths that support you throughout your journey. Every number in your birth date indicates the types of opportunities and lessons you will experience.

Numerology is also:

o   A study of human nature – how we make our way in the world, how we relate to others, and our basic psychological and emotional make-up

o   A study of profound universal truths that assist us in our growth and evolution

o   A metaphysical framework for examining our Sacred Contract

o   A system for proactive living that offers guidance and can help us to plan for success in all that we undertake

Numerology will help you determine the right approach and the right time for everything, from visiting your mother to planning a career move or finding your romantic soul-mate.

How to Use This Book

You will find it very helpful to use a journal or the note pages that are included in this book for your calculations and for answering the reflective questions. Although the book is designed for you to read on your own, you will also enjoy reading it with a partner or a group of friends or co-workers, so that you can compare your experiences with each number, and discuss your answers to the questions.

To determine your personal numbers you will start with some very simple calculations. These will give you the numbers of your personal year, month, and day.

The Personal Year section describes the way in which the number of your temporary vibration affects the main areas of your life—career, finances, relationships, and personal growth—for the entire year from one birthday to the next. There are proactive choices listed for each of your personal years, to show you how you can make the best use of that year's numeric energy. There is also a suggested affirmation for each of your personal years.

The Personal Month explains how the numeric energy will affect your life over a period of a few weeks during, and within the context of your personal year. This section indicates what types of issues, themes, or events are likely to arise and what types of short term projects are most favoured during your month. Information in the personal month section is relevant to all aspects of your life, including career and romance. There is also a section that will tell you when you can expect the energy of your personal month to support, complement, or intensify the energy of your personal year. (As proactive choices would be redundant at this point, you are encouraged to refer to the proactive choices that are listed with each personal year number and modify them for the shorter period of time.)

The Personal Day section explains the way in which the numbers 1 to 9, and the master numbers 11, 22, and 33, affect your day to day reality. It provides examples of the kinds of interactions, activities and events that you may be intuitively drawn to, and that are likely to arise in your life that day.

This section also indicates some of the pitfalls of your personal day number. Each number represents a continuum of attributes. When the energy of that number is expressed at a lower level on the continuum, we may be drawn to actions or thought processes that ultimately diminish our sense of security

4

and self-worth. Awareness is the most important tool we can use to keep our vibrations running high and our energy strong.

Since the purpose of this book is to show readers how to use the energy of their temporary vibration to its best possible advantage, there is a list of proactive choices for each day. These are suggestions for activities and initiatives that are favoured and enhanced by your personal day number, and that will, in turn, add greater value to your life and your experience of that number. They are meant to guide you in planning your day, your work, and your leisure activities, to align with the progression of your nine day "week", but not to dictate how you must live your life.

By scheduling certain activities to align with the energy of your personal day, you will meet with less resistance, stress, and frustration. You will gain a greater sense of purpose and accomplishment, as well as greater restorative benefit from your leisure activities. Whenever you participate in a soul-enhancing activity, the benefit to yourself and others is ongoing.

NOTE: Not all proactive choices need to be followed each time you have a particular day, but by following some of these suggestions, you will find that the energy of that number is flowing, that you feel more in charge of situations and circumstances, and, quite likely, that you are getting more enjoyment out of life.

Many readers live with a partner, spouse, and or children. There is a section with each personal day to show you how you can enhance the personal day of those you care for, even when you are experiencing a different number yourself.

Finally there is a section for single people to show them how the personal day may be used to help them find a romantic partner.

Not every aspect of your personal day number will present itself in a given twenty-four hour period; but, at the end of the day, as you reflect on events and activities within the context of your personal number, you are likely to find that several elements of that energy that have come forward at different times during your day, or that one particular element has been dominant.

Make notes over a period of two or three nine day cycles. If possible, compare your findings with the experiences of one or more of your friends or co-workers. Don't try to make the number fit or to make your experiences fit the number. You won't need to do that because after you have worked with your

Personal Number System for a short period of time, you will start to feel its rhythm, to get "in sync" with the logical progression from one to nine.

For each personal year number, as well as each personal day number, you will find brief stories that illustrate the numbers at work in peoples' lives. Some of these are my own personal experiences and some are experiences that my clients have had. In the latter case, the names have been changed.

Cycles within Cycles

Before we examine in detail what each of the numbers brings to our personal year, month, and day, we need to clarify the term "cycles". What are cycles and how do they affect us?

The waxing and waning of the moon, the ebb and flow of the ocean's tides, the miracle of transformation that brings a beautiful butterfly out of its cocoon, the progression of our personal year, right through to our solar return, the progression of our personal months and days—each of these represents a cycle, and each is an example of Divine Perfection.

The longest cycle of our journey is the life path. This is our cycle from birth to death. There are also shorter cycles in our journey, and these we refer to as temporary vibrations. They are with us for a period of time. It may be as long as thirty years, as in a major cycle, or nine years, as in a second or third pinnacle.

When we examine these cycles using the science of numerology, we see that they are periods of time when themes and issues emerge and re-emerge. We become aware of the progress that we are making within each cycle, and are able to see how these patterns of energy move us forward in terms of our personal growth, our soul's evolution, and indeed the evolution of our entire global family.

There are several excellent books, listed in the bibliography, which explain your life path, major cycles, and pinnacles in detail. Those topics are beyond the scope of this book, which is dealing exclusively with the shorter cycles.

The Shortest Cycle

In this book, we will calculate and examine your personal year and month, before looking very closely at the shortest cycle of all, the personal day.

Why is the largest part of this book about the shortest cycle?

... Because it's the days in our lives and specifically the moments in our days that carry the most meaning for us, that create the greatest impact on our soul's growth.

... Because when we are spending our time wisely each day we are better able to minimize stress and maintain a positive level of Life Force Energy.

... Because when we minimize stress, we have greater Peace of Mind. We are in the flow. When we are "in the flow", we contribute to the well-being of everyone on the planet.

That is not to say that with this system, every day will be filled with sunshine and roses! Not every day can be that way, but every day brings blessings, many blessings, and opportunities to engage in the process of life and to fully participate in your soul's growth.

In his book, "The Life You Were Born to Live",[1] author Dan Millman uses the term "ride the crest of the wave". Each of us may find different ways to ride the crest of the wave, but ultimately it will always mean that we are living consciously, in harmony with the numerical energy that is with us for each day, and finding ways, moment to moment, to use our time wisely and contribute to the highest good of our planet and our fellow human beings.

All it takes to understand the energy of your personal day - and to work effectively with the energy of all your temporary vibrations - is a basic understanding of the nature of each number, and some simple addition exercises!

---

1   Millman, Dan, The Life You Were Born to Live, AJ Kramer,& New World Library; Novato CA 1993

Part Two
Begin with Your
Personal Year

Your Personal Year

Knowing the number of your year helps you to understand the major events and developments that occur in your personal and professional life. It brings validation and encouragement, and helps to prepare you for upcoming lessons and blessings.

What is a Personal Year?

Personal years are regular, progressive cycles that bring forward certain themes and opportunities. The energy of your personal year tends to be highly discernible, and you'll usually feel as though your life is revolving around a certain theme or perhaps a certain project. For example you may:

- ○ Start a new job

- ○ Go back to school

- ○ Start a business

- ○ End a relationship

- ○ Start a relationship

- ○ Have a baby

- ○ Buy, or build a house…

The situations that arise during your personal year will be congruent with the energy of that particular number, and very often the actions that you initiate will instinctively be those that are supported by the numeric energy of your year.

The energetic patterns of the personal year are repeated over and over again every nine years throughout our lives. Although we repeat the numbers over and over, a great deal of learning occurs along the way.

Nine years later, when we experience the same number of personal year once more, our lives will be different and our souls will be at a higher level of evolution than they were during the previous year that we encountered that same numerical influence. We gain even more benefit from the number than we did nine years before. If you think of a circular path winding around a mountain, you'll keep coming back to the same side of the mountain but you'll always be higher up.

It is true that some people do not acknowledge their spirituality, or simply cannot summon the will to break free from negative patterns and self-sabotage. For these people, the learning becomes much more difficult and the growth is minimal, but it still occurs. The numbers are at work in everyone's life, regardless of whether they choose to accept the gifts or not.

Although the personal year begins on your birthday, there is a transition period. For a few weeks before your birthday you will feel your focus shifting as a new theme begins to emerge.

How to Calculate Your Personal Year

To calculate your own personal year, start with the number of the month that you were born.

Use the numbers 10, 11, and 12 for October, November, and December respectively. We don't reduce those numbers until later in the calculation.

Then add to that the number of the day that you were born.

Then add the number of the calendar year for your last birthday.

For example if your last birthday was in 2011, you would add the number 4 (2+1+1) to the number you got when combining your day and month. If the birthday was in 2012 you would add 5; in 2013, 6; and so on.

Eliminate the zeros from your calculation; we are adding only the digits 1 to 9.

You will end up with a two digit number. If that number is 11, 22, or 33, it is a master number, and must be left that way. All other two digit numbers will be added together to get only one digit.

For example:

At this writing, the year is 2011.

If your birthday was on December 31, and you are doing this calculation on or after January 1 of the next year, you will use the number of the previous calendar year, 2010.

Your calculation will look like this:

12+31+3=46

Then you must add the 4 and 6 together.

4+6=10

You must now eliminate the zero, and you find that, on your last birthday, you began a 1 personal year.

You will continue to be in a 1 year until your next birthday, at which time the calculation will be:

12+31+4=47

4+7=11

Below are two more examples:

This birthday was on September 11, 2011

The calculation looks like this:

9+11+4=24

2+4=6

This person is in a 6 personal year until her next birthday in September of 2012.

Please Take a Number

This birthday was on April 8, 2011.

The calculation looks like this:

4+8+4=16

1+6=7

This person will be in a 7 personal year until her next birthday in April of 2012.

Once you have finished your calculations, the following pages will tell you about the indications and proactive choices for your personal year.

Your 1 Personal Year

Focus: You and Your Journey

If you are in a 1 personal year, you are beginning a new nine year cycle. This is a time to be creative and innovative, to take action, and follow new opportunities that will come your way. There is work to be done, as you are laying new foundations and opening up to new opportunities.

Decisive Action and a New Career

Dena had her degree in education, but she had been a stay at home mother for many years. As her children got older she began to regret the fact that she hadn't developed a career. She spent a lot of time reflecting on her own needs and aspirations, as well as taking inventory of her strengths and abilities. She then surprised her family by taking a quick and very intensive course that would qualify her to teach English as a second language. Before her year was over she had found a part time position with her local school board. Dena loves meeting adult students from all over the world and making a difference in their lives. She also values the independence and sense of personal power that her new career has given her.

This is usually an excellent time to make a career move. Whether you initiate the move yourself or not, it is highly likely that you will meet a new boss or mentor in your 1 year. There is also a strong possibility that you will step into a leadership role.

A leadership role will often bring financial increase. While some increase in salary is likely, some of this increase could come as a larger package of benefits, stock options, or a better pension plan. Because this is the 1 year there is the sense that you are sowing seeds that will bear fruit later on.

Have courage, make plans, and avoid indecision. Focus on yourself, and be selfish in the healthiest sense of that word. At some point this year you may be required to face a challenging situation on your own. You will take pride in being self-reliant.

Although we often experience endings in a 9 year, it's possible that abrupt endings may occur in certain areas of your life in your 1 year as well. Some of the endings that occur in a 1 year seem to come as a result of external circumstances, and some from our own personal choices. For example, you may wish to extricate yourself from an employment or housing situation that is not serving your highest good. Avoid being impulsive or headstrong, yet be willing to change for the sake of your own personal progress and happiness.

Any relationships that are no longer valid for you may have ended in your previous (9) year; but, if not, they may end abruptly in your 1 year. With a stronger desire for independence this year, you may actually choose to initiate the ending. This need never be done unkindly, and is always a blessing for all concerned.

This is an auspicious time to begin new relationships and make new connections for personal or business reasons. People who enter your circle in a 1 personal year will play a significant role for many years to come. They may become romantic partners, close friends, or mentors. Marriage ties can be strengthened in a 1 year. In terms of romance, sometimes the 1 offers the delightful opportunity for friends to become lovers, and lovers to become friends.

Proactive Choices for Your 1 Personal Year

Take inventory of your personal strengths and talents.

Focus your attention on one goal at a time.

In goal planning, develop a clear picture of your desired outcome.

Use your journal to write about and refine your vision for the lifestyle you would like to achieve.

Become familiar with, and make use of metaphysical principles of manifestation.

Savour new experiences and activities.

Remain open to invitations and opportunities to meet new people.

Schedule quality time for yourself.

Affirmation:

I am a channel for creative and original ideas.

Your 2 Personal Year

Focus: Your Close Relationships

The 2 year tends to be more restful and reflective. After the force and movement of the 9 and 1 years, the 2 offers opportunities to integrate change, and to settle into new routines or a new environment. It is not a time of dramatic change or progress, but it is a good year to consolidate gains that have been made in your 1 year.

Settling In

Joan had spent her 1 year orchestrating a long distance move to the west coast. She had taken on most of the responsibilities and details involved in purchasing a new home, moving, and establishing her son in his new school, while her husband stayed behind to ensure a smooth transition of their successful business to new owners.

It had definitely been a year of daunting "to-do" lists, but the end result was well worth it. Now in her 2 year, Joan is happily settling into her new surroundings, making new friends in the community, and enjoying life near the ocean. For now she is traveling from time to time between the two locations; but, before her 2 year is over, her husband will join her in their new home.

Any projects, relationships or business deals that were initiated last year will either begin to "gel"; or, if they are not in your best interests, it will become increasingly clear that there is a lack of energetic support from the Universe. Generally in the 2 year there is a spirit of cooperation and a willingness to compromise. It is a time for team work and collaboration, a time to support others, to seek out role models and be receptive to learning from them.

Business partnerships or collaborative endeavours are favoured in the 2 year. It is time to share your plans and seek association, for mutual benefit, with one or two trustworthy individuals who will lend support to your initiative. In return, others will be coming to you this year for similar support. You are required to conduct all of your personal and professional affairs with consideration, co-operation, diplomacy, and attention to detail.

Financial gain is not usually substantial in a 2 year, but careful planning and attention to details can help you make slow but steady progress. You will feel guided to save money this year, and to account for each dollar that is spent.

People who are in relationships tend to turn their attention to the quality of these relationships. Are your needs for respect, attention, intimacy, and practical or moral support being addressed? Anything that is not serving the highest good for you and/or your partner will become glaring and obvious, and could result in a breakup.

Your personal magnetism is growing stronger. If you are single you may long for the comfort of quiet companionship, and may, in fact, attract a new partner into your life at this time.

Proactive Choices for Your 2 Personal Year

Spend quality time with your significant other.

Resolve any existing conflict and strengthen your relationships, just as the spider strengthens and repairs each strand in her web.

Look for ways to support others in attaining their goals.

Seek balance in all areas of your life, including physical activity and rest, work and play, time with others and time alone.

Small social gatherings are more appropriate this year, rather than large parties.

Establish personal boundaries, learn to say no, and do not become a doormat.

Remain open to new ties, alliances, and support networks.

Take care of details, and read the fine print in any agreements that you sign.

Affirmation:

I enjoy mutual respect and harmony in all my relationships.

Your 3 Personal Year

Focus: Expansion and Fulfillment

By the time the 3 year comes around, you are likely to be in a very sociable mood. You are much more visible to others this year, and working with the public is favoured. (In fact it is an excellent campaign year for aspiring politicians.) There is an element of popularity, with both large and small groups, and you find that several invitations are coming your way.

There is a higher level of interest in the visual and performing arts this year, and you may in fact be creating some fine work of art yourself. Creativity and self expression is a very strong element this year, and it is a good time to write articles or a book, and to present speeches. Be diligent in what you say, write, and sign. When it comes to any type of agreement, be sure to read the fine print or listen carefully to make sure that you understand.

This can be a good year for selling products, (including your writing), or services. To an extent you are in the spotlight. Others will become more aware of your talents, and there could be a promotion before the end of this year.

On the Campaign Trail

President Barack Obama was in his 3 personal year for most of 2008. This added extra momentum to his presidential campaign, as he traveled all over the United States meeting people, expressing his ideas, showcasing his presentation skills, and gaining support. In particular, the 3 energy made him look good and enhanced his connection with younger voters. By the time he was elected president, he was in a 22 personal year. In fact, the election took place the day he began his 33 personal month.

Plan to take a vacation, particularly one with an artistic focus, such as photography, painting, writing, or even visiting art galleries or attending plays. Both men and women may wish to try a new hairstyle or buy some new clothes, as we become more interested in our appearance at this time. Romance and affection are highlighted during this cycle. In fact, speaking of romance, the 3 is a number of fertility, so for younger couples, it also favours pregnancy.

21

As the number of the inner child, the 3 can sometimes bring forward issues from childhood that have not yet been resolved, or relationships with parents and siblings that need to be healed. If that happens these may arise in the form of a crisis, as the wounded child starts to cry out for attention. A crisis can be such a gift, because it means that something we have tolerated for far too long is now being dealt with and resolved.

You will need to be diligent about your budget, as it is easy to overspend in a 3 year. The 3 can be a lucky year if your efforts and financial resources are not scattered and your energies are focused on priority goals. During this year you must watch that you bring projects to completion before beginning something new.

Proactive Choices for Your 3 Personal Year

Allow your inner child to play.

Keep track of your expenses, especially while on vacation.

Host small and larger parties, and spend time with friends and family.

Take every opportunity to meet new people.

Learn a new language.

Express yourself in creative ways.

Listen to music, attend concerts, or play an instrument.

Join a choir or singing group.

Give your time, energy, and affection to those who are deserving.

Share your skills, wisdom, and insight through teaching, speaking, and/or writing.

Affirmation:

I place myself in the path of magic this year, and hold positive expectations.

Your 4 Personal Year

Focus: Long Term Security

Play time is over now, and it's possible that, as you move into your 4 year, you are looking forward to creating more structure and organization in your life. Even if you are normally inclined to challenge parameters and conventions, you will have a more conservative mindset in a 4 year.

There is a greater sense of practicality and you are putting a lot of energy into your career and long term security. For example, in the 4 year you may buy some land with the view to building in the near future, or you may actually begin the task of building a house. This is a year to build a foundation, make important connections, concentrate on the task at hand, and take incremental steps toward goal attainment.

Expansion in a 4 year is typically slow and steady, but positive. It is entirely likely that you will feel restricted to some degree. Think of the old saying, "when fishermen can't go to sea, they mend their nets". This is your opportunity to consolidate and retrench, as your life will become very active and expansive in the year to follow.

You may put in a lot of extra hours at work, and it will not go unnoticed by either your own boss, or someone else who may offer you a new position, with even greater responsibility. Opportunities for career advancement often come toward the end of a 4 year. You may be approached by "head hunters" or a prospective employer.

If you are in business for yourself, you will be working steadily and will likely feel guided to review and prioritize long range goals. Financial goals are attainable but once again there will not be dramatic gains. You will be careful about your expenses and will likely feel guided to put extra money into long term savings or investments, or to accelerate your debt reduction.

In your personal life, you are concerned with strength, security, and stability for yourself and your family. Your resolve is strong and you take commitments to yourself and others seriously. The 4 is a good year for engagement and marriage, a good year to follow a routine, pay off debts, start a diet, or quit smoking. In other words, you are well advised to get your house in order in terms of relationships, body, mind, and spirit.

Added Responsibility and Time in Nature

Scott had just begun his 4 year when he accepted a voluntary position on the board of a not-for-profit children's camp. This new commitment added a lot of extra work to his schedule and it also gave him an opportunity to spend time in nature and promote his passion for sound environmental stewardship. Another positive development in his 4 year was that he moved out of his rental apartment and purchased a home of his own.

If, in calculating your 4 personal year, your double digit number is 13, the indication is that you are in a two year period of drastic change and expansion. Some outmoded way of thinking, being, or relating to the world is being left behind, and you are in a process of reinventing your life.

Naturally this is not as steady and predictable as a 4 year that comes from the double digits 31 or 40. Like the typical 4 year, your focus will be on your foundation and your long-term security; and you will be working very hard to achieve that goal.

However, unlike the 4 year, there is a strong possibility that you will be trying to process and integrate constantly changing circumstances. It is not uncommon in a 13 year to receive a gift that is initially disguised as a loss. The 13 is a number of transformation and regeneration.

Proactive Choices for Your 4 Personal Year

Meet key people who can strengthen your initiative.

Exercise caution and gather information when making decisions - this is not a good year to take major risks.

Give some time and attention to security for your home and belongings.

Do necessary maintenance and repairs.

Seek out results and a worthwhile reason for your effort.

Review, reflect, and take care of anything that has been overlooked.

Pay attention to details.

Review your financial situation.

Spend time in nature.

Begin and maintain an exercise and nutrition program.

Pay attention to your personal boundaries.

Strengthen your family unit.

In a 13 year add the following proactive choices:

Keep a journal to record your thoughts, feelings, and creative ideas.

Spend time with positive people who are sensible as well as open-minded.

Monitor your health and manage stress levels.

Affirmation:

I now apply self discipline and due diligence in all areas of my life, and am grateful for positive results.

Your 5 Personal Year

Focus: Activity and Change

We are constantly changing and developing; that is the essence of life itself. Now that it is your 5 personal year, the changes that are underway will be dramatic and probably life altering. They will definitely be noticeable to others.

Changes that often occur in a 5 year may include, but are not necessarily limited to, a change in relationship status, a career change, relocation to another city, a business failure, a business success, a financial setback, a financial increase, or a pregnancy. Obviously, this can be a time of upheaval, and it is possible that more than one crisis will command your attention. Always remember that in the Chinese alphabet, the characters for crisis are literally translated as "Danger + Opportunity".

Not all change needs to bring distress. Do not enter into your 5 personal year with a sense of foreboding. The 5 is a very progressive number, and it is possible that there may be pleasant surprises and opportunities in store for you at this time. To reap the benefit of these opportunities, you will need to remain positive and optimistic in your outlook. Make good use of the Law of Attraction as the 5 year is a time when it can work very well for you.

This is the number of freedom and expansion, and you will be driven by a desire to break free from your usual routine, to delve into unknown areas, and to reconstruct your life in a way that feels more authentic to you. It's a time to be open to anything in terms of your personal and professional goals. Accept no limitations. You may do a complete career change, one that involves not just who you work for but also how you make your living.

Following My Passion

I was in a 5 personal year when I left my position as a school teacher to follow my passion for spirituality and holistic healing. It was a difficult year as I dealt with a larger than usual number of students with learning disabilities and behavioural challenges. Unfortunately the teachers went on strike that year and my cash flow was impacted. After the strike was settled, I became ill, had surgery, and was unable to finish the school year with my students. That was also the year that I began doing Reiki and talking to people about numerology, the year that the Universe gave me the gift of a new career path and an entirely new group of "kindred spirits".

After making well-informed decisions, it is appropriate to take action in a 5 year. It is also appropriate to express yourself (particularly through writing, as 5 is the number of the scribe), and to seek out new people, new places and new situations. You may be called upon to give up certain roles and relationships, and certain aspects of your current reality, in order to make greater gains in terms of fulfilling your potential. Ultimately the choice will be yours. Know that you are never asked to turn away from the essence of your being, just to make adjustments that will take you to greater happiness in the long run.

Proactive Choices for Your 5 Personal Year

Remain open to innovative ways of doing your work.

Take advantage of opportunities to meet new people.

Read travel brochures and if possible consider a destination that you've never been to before.

Take up a new hobby, and/or seek out a "meet-up" group in some area that interests you.

Work toward balance in terms of honouring your need for personal space and freedom, while maintaining your relationships and responsibilities to others.

Within reason and using good judgement, be willing to give up certain elements of your current life, in order to work toward your highest potential.

Gather information and take time to make your decisions, considering all long-term implications.

Keep fit, and practice moderation in terms of food, and drink.

Bring colour into your wardrobe and environment.

Avoid excessive spending and use of credit cards.

Work with the Law of Attraction, and expect the best for yourself and others.

Affirmation:

I now attract people, circumstances and finances to make my dreams come true.

Your 6 Personal Year

Focus: Responsibility

If you are in a 6 personal year, you are surrounded by benevolent, protective influences. Your energy is directed toward the home front, and it's possible that certain members of your family, or some of your close friends, need your help. It is a time to counsel, console, guide, and give assistance to family members and friends. You probably feel emotionally involved, and, you may even feel that you are "spread thin" as you provide comfort and support to others.

Your relationships with those near and dear to you are likely to grow even closer and stronger this year. This may be a relationship with your parents, children, or siblings, or it may be with a romantic partner. The 6 is an auspicious year to begin a marriage, or to welcome a new baby; however, you need to know that if things are not going well in any of your current relationships, especially with your spouse or partner, the issues will rise to the surface now. They will either be resolved, or the relationship will end.

You may have some projects in mind for your home, perhaps decorating, buying furniture, or even finding a new home. Plan to personalize your environment with family photographs, fresh flowers, or treasured objects and artefacts.

Because this is a year of learning, balance, and harmony, it would be to your benefit to engage in any activity or discipline that focuses on your own well being and balance. If you have ever wanted to take new and interesting courses, or fulfill a desire to paint, sing, act, or play a musical instrument for pleasure, this is a favourable year to do so.

This is not normally a year that we associate with career movement, although sometimes in a 6 year people start a home-based business or continue working for their current employer from a home office.

It is definitely a year when common sense prevails in all areas of your life, including your finances. You are not likely to receive a large increase; however, it is likely that you will be in a good position to contribute to your savings, and that you will have a better sense of control over your expenses than you had in your 5 year.

Real Estate and Relationships

Louise was going through a divorce in her 6 year. She was unsure about whether she wanted to keep her large home, so she rented it out and moved into a charming little house by the ocean. As it turned out, her idyllic little beach house had a serious problem with mould, and she began feeling ill almost immediately after moving. With tenants in her own home, she had no choice but to move in with her boyfriend for a period of several months, until her tenants' lease was up. The arrangement worked very well, and although she is not ready to make it permanent, she is glad that she had this opportunity in her 6 year to further develop her relationship with the new man in her life.

Proactive Choices for Your 6 Personal Year

Give some time and attention to security for your home and belongings.

Renovate or redecorate your personal space.

Buy yourself some comfortable and attractive lounging clothes for cozy nights at home.

Personalize your work environment with one or two plants, and a few treasured photographs.

Visit an art gallery.

Practice yoga, T'ai Chi, or meditation.

Seek harmony in your personal relationships; work to resolve issues and strengthen communication.

Respect other peoples' boundaries and avoid being a "rescuer".

Gracefully release relationships that are not in your best interest.

Strive to attain a position of comfort, balance, and peace of mind.

Remember; "It's hard to spread sunshine without getting a little on yourself."

Affirmation:

I create beauty and harmony for myself and others.

Your 7 Personal Year

Focus: Solitude and Acceptance

Your 7 year has the potential to bring you to a place of peace, reassurance, and acceptance of all the lessons and blessings that life has brought your way. If you honour the introspective nature of the 7, you will increase your understanding of yourself, find that you are better able to solve problems, and come to a greater awareness of your full potential. By the end of this year you will likely be in a position to handle life with greater insight and efficiency.

This is meant to be an inner year, a year of study and reflection, a time to analyze your thoughts and actions, and pursue topics of an intellectual or metaphysical nature. You are most likely feeling the urge to explore life's deeper truths, either by looking into philosophical matters or possibly by studying natural sciences. This may mean that you will choose to go back to school, to work on a degree or at least pursue some type of formal and structured learning. It could also mean that you will instead go to seminars and otherwise engage in some type of self guided study in an area that interests you.

You must now detach from ego and emotions as you begin to take an analytical look at your progress so far. There may be financial constraints in a 7 year; but all your needs will be met. Strengthen your faith. Avoid striving. This is not a year to go after things with force and determination; but, it is the perfect time to surrender to the Universe and let everything work out according to Divine timing.

There will definitely be limits on your social activity. For example, sometimes in a 7 year people are recuperating from a lengthy illness or adjusting to life without a loved one who has recently died. On a less heart-wrenching note, it can also be a time when your partner has taken a night job or is working out of town, or a close friend has just moved to another city. Connections that you have established will endure, but right now you need a rest, so embrace this energy and welcome your time alone.

This is not usually a year for career movement, although through your studies you are gaining expertise that will serve you well in terms of your professional status. In a 7 year sometimes people take on a position as a trouble shooter, analyst, or business advisor. Sometimes promotions are offered near the end of a 7 year, as others begin to recognize your expertise.

More Time Alone

Jane's husband had been unemployed for several long months. It was the beginning of her 7 year when he found a position as a night auditor in a boutique hotel. This meant that he was sleeping most of the afternoon and evening, and gone all night. Their social life as a couple was almost non-existent and Jane ate dinner alone almost every night for a year until her husband found another job with regular daytime hours.

Proactive Choices for Your 7 Personal Year

Keep a journal.

Keep your surroundings tidy and well organized.

Keep social activities low key and ensure that you have plenty of time alone.

Learn to be alone without being lonely.

Gather useful information, but maintain confidentiality.

Establish routines that include time for prayer and meditation.

Go to bed early and make sure you get plenty of rest.

Participate in activities that will restore and replenish your energy.

Read books about philosophy or metaphysical studies.

Further develop your position as an expert in your field.

Do not undertake new initiatives, unless they involve taking classes or pursuing academic goals.

Examine your financial position and evaluate your spending and saving patterns.

Set positive intentions and maintain your faith that the Universe will deliver.

Affirmation:

I am in the right place, at the right time, for the right purpose.

Your 8 Personal Year

Focus: Career

The transition from one year to the next can sometimes seem quite dramatic. In your 8 year you have moved in a major way from the spiritual realm of wisdom and introspection, into the very earthly realm of material concerns. The ideas and insight that came to you during the 7 year are now ready to be tested in the harsh light of practicality.

Think Big! This is a perfect time to refine a grand vision for who you want to become and what you hope to accomplish. Emotional involvements may take a back burner this year, as you focus on prosperity and career advancement; however, it is always in your best interest to place value on your close relationships and to devote a measure of your time and attention to your loved ones.

You may notice a competitive side to your nature, and if you are involved in athletic pursuits you will reap the benefits of increased strength and drive. The 8 year calls upon you to be decisive, take action, and step into leadership roles. You will come into contact with people who carry a great deal of influence in your particular line of work. If they are individuals who are known for both their accomplishments and their contributions, consider them to be role models. They are reflecting qualities that you yourself possess, or they wouldn't be in your life.

If you are working for someone else, you will probably be offered a promotion this year, along with a raise and a substantial increase in your responsibilities. If you are self-employed you will also notice an increase in revenue and work assignments. You are in a position to contribute much to the success of any business enterprise that you are involved with.

As you work with the Law of Attraction, you will notice that your ability to manifest is strengthened. You are in a position to reap the rewards of previous efforts and productivity. When individuals have not been diligent with their work, or have not developed an understanding of the universal laws that govern prosperity, the 8 year can bring about financial challenges. You will be receiving and spending larger amounts of money this year. As long as you have been practicing due diligence, and are mindfully following proven money management principles, you will be in a better financial position at the end of your year.

Greater Control and Financial Increase

After years of mounting debts, Laura, a single woman in her fifties, admitted that she was out of control. She started paying for everything with cash, and made tough decisions that helped her to trim some of her expenses. She also saw a financial planner and started paying down her debts.

At the same time she chose to apply diligent effort to a business that she had started with a multi-level marketing company. Laura's efforts paid off. Her business began to grow, and she is enjoying financial increase and a greater sense of personal power.

Force, energy, and authentic power are at your command this year. You are called to use it with integrity and wisdom, and to hold positive intentions for the greatest good of everyone concerned.

Proactive Choices for Your 8 Personal Year

Write your goals. . . Dream big!

Develop sound strategies for attaining your goals.

Plan ahead and be mindful of how you manage your time.

Combine passion and commitment with decisive action.

Consider the phrase personal best, what it would mean for you, what it would look like, feel like, sound like, and how you would recognize it.

Think always in terms of what you would like to do, have, and be.

Keep a success journal.

Consider taking a course in public speaking.

Be open to upgrading your knowledge and skills in the area of financial planning or anything else to do with money.

Use distraction and physical activity to avoid periods of depression.

Use positive self-talk to maintain a high level of confidence.

Affirmation:

I gratefully accept success, recognition, and abundance in return for my skill and effort.

Your 9 Personal Year

Focus: Release and Closure

This is your year of endings, a time of completion and release. It is the most important year of your nine year cycle. You are bringing to a conclusion what you have learned and created in the previous eight years and completely integrating it into your present life.

This year you are getting ready for change and new beginnings, and cannot be burdened by what belongs to your past. You must take a critical look at all areas of your life, to see what is no longer valid. Anything that no longer contributes to your growth and enlightenment, or to your enjoyment of life, must be released with grace and gratitude. This process of discrimination will, of necessity, take place on several levels.

This is a year of movement and change, when you may be required to let go of a romantic relationship, a friendship, a job, or even a home that no longer serves your greatest good. If you are approaching mid-life this could be the year that one or more of your children leave home. In keeping with the emotional nature of the number 9, it may also be a year when you will need to say good-bye to a loved one who is leaving the Earth plane, or when you will need to confront a painful memory and do some major work in the area of release and forgiveness.

You may face a temporary loss of income this year, or find that your finances are up and down for a short period of time. Someone in your family may approach you for a loan, or one of your children may ask for money. If your financial situation remains stable, you may feel guided to give a generous donation to a charity of your choice.

Loss, Release, Forgiveness

For many years Jodi had been a highly successful sales associate with a furniture company. She lost her job, and it was several uncomfortable weeks before she was offered a new position at another store. Unfortunately her new co-workers felt threatened by Jodi's outgoing personality as well as her skill and experience, and the dynamics in her workplace became toxic. In emotional turmoil, as we sometimes are in a 9 year, she left her second workplace and went to yet another furniture dealer. The third store turned out to be disorganized and unreliable, and Jodi very quickly realized that she had made a disastrous decision. She was met with great resistance from her former supervisor when she tried to go back to the second store.

That same year, Jodi honoured her healing gifts and became a Reiki practitioner. Rather than giving in to fear or resentment, she sent Reiki, loving thoughts, and pure white light to her former co-workers and supervisor. Eventually this lady relented, and agreed to take her back onto the sales team. She actually told Jodi that after this first-hand experience, she would never doubt the benefit of sending healing energy. Jodi continues to use her healing gifts in this way. She has noticed a difference in her workplace dynamics, and now feels that she is a valued member of her team.

In terms of your career you may be working more in the public arena this year, and your work may have a broader impact. You may actually leave a job, although any new position that you take on, particularly in the first half of a 9 year, will most likely be a "stepping stone" that will take you to another situation in (or closer to) your 1 year.

A 9 year often brings a wide variety of experiences and opportunities. You will likely have at least one opportunity to travel abroad. If this is not the case, then you will be meeting people from other parts of the world. Any artistic endeavours that you undertake will be enhanced by the energy of this personal year. As the number of completion, the 9 helps you to complete the cycle of giving and receiving. It is not uncommon at this time to enjoy the benefits of good karma, and to receive gifts along with expressions of deep appreciation.

You will be required to let go of ego-based attachments, and to serve others with deep compassion. The paradox of this year is that although it often seems to drain your physical, mental and emotional stamina, it is also a time when deep healing can occur for you. By far the most effective way to handle the 9 year is to practice spiritual surrender, to embrace the energy and become consciously engaged in the process of change.

If you have done the work of the 9 year, the transition period into your 1 year brings a sense of freedom, enjoyment and awakening.

Proactive Choices for Your 9 Personal Year

Avoid beginning major projects, such as going back to school, building a house, starting a business etc.

Examine your thought processes, and behavioural patterns to see if there is anything that no longer serves your greatest good.

Divulge personal or business information only on a need to know basis.

Release any relationships that are no longer of mutual benefit.

It's time to PURGE. Go through closets and cupboards and get rid of any belongings that you no longer use or enjoy.

Take a vacation.

Take advantage of opportunities to go to concerts, plays, or art galleries.

Seek medical attention for any health concerns.

Explore alternative or complementary therapies.

Work with your angels for protection, healing, and forgiveness.

Affirmations:

I willingly release that which I no longer need, to make way for new and greater good.

Master Numbers

There are times when we do not "reduce" to one digit. That is when adding your day, month, and the current calendar year gives you a total of 11, 22, or 33. These are called master numbers. They bring powerful energy, rigorous requirements, and potential for rich rewards. Each of us will experience the energy of an 11 personal year, (instead of a 2 year) at some point during our lives. Many of us will also experience the energy of a 22 personal year instead of a 4 year. The 33 year, which would take the place of a 6 personal year, is not as common.

Your 11 Personal Year

Focus: Truth and Priorities

If you are currently in an 11 personal year, your intuition is likely working overtime, with visions, flashes of insight, and psychic illumination bringing new opportunities for spiritual growth. Important books will somehow find their way into your hands, and you will meet more and more people who, like you, are on a soulful path. You may decide to take courses or join a study group. Inspired thinking, originality, and inventiveness, may culminate in a writing project or an artistic endeavour. Meditation will be deeply fulfilling, but keep yourself grounded by eating well, using crystals, such as hematite, or by getting out into natural surroundings.

Sometimes the 11 year can bring stressful situations, sudden twists and turns in the plot, and unexpected associations or unexpected breakups. Regardless of the way your 11 year unfolds and the surprising developments that may seem to come from "out of the blue", you will be presented with an opportunity to achieve much success in pursuit of both your personal goals and your professional aspirations. The 11 year will call upon you to examine your priorities, and possibly to make a sudden change of direction based upon new information and insight. In fact you may take sudden action that will surprise you as much as it surprises everyone around you. You won't be thinking "outside the box", you'll be nowhere near the box. Your life, your surroundings, your circle of friends and associates will never look the same.

Surprising Everyone

Angela had lived in a western city for more than thirty years. Her marriage had ended many years ago and her sons had grown up and moved away - one to Toronto and one to Vancouver. She was tired of her surroundings and of her small one bedroom apartment condo, and she had recently retired from her job as a school librarian.

Looking for a new beginning, she decided to move east. Unfortunately this coincided with a stagnant real estate market, and after several discouraging months she decided that pursuing her dream was more important than sticking to her price. She also knew that she would get more for her money at the other end.

She dropped her asking price by $40,000.00, which came as a shock to her realtor and her friends. Within a week her apartment was sold, and she had all she needed to start her new life. Things happened very quickly from that point and within a few weeks Angela was enjoying a back yard, extra room, and a new life in her home near her son in Toronto.

The 11 year can bring financial setbacks, but it can also bring positive developments. For example, you may be able to add another stream of income, profit from your investments, or manifest increased revenue in some other way. New information and original ideas will inspire you to set priorities and help you to gain focus, clarity, and a sense of direction in your financial matters.

In terms of your personal life, you are highly visible and sought after by family members and friends who admire you, and welcome your input and energetic support for their own initiatives.

With personal magnetism at its peak, you will widen your sphere of influence. You are in the spotlight, and others are aware of what you have to contribute to the success of their enterprise. This is a favourable time to launch an innovative new product, invention, or service. There is a lot of power at your command, and if you choose to use it wisely, it can bring outstanding results and accomplishments. Keep in mind that to be truly enduring, your growth in all areas must include service to others.

If you maintain your focus, the 11 can be a "Go For It" year!

Proactive Choices for Your 11 Personal Year

Live in the moment, and experience the energies around you with conscious awareness.

Be mindful of the effects of your surroundings, particularly if there is loud music or vulgar language.

Avoid news, or violent, depressing movies. Anything that comes through electronic or print media will affect your nerves this year.

Be kind and gentle with yourself and others as your level of understanding increases.

You are highly receptive to positive energy. See an energy healing practitioner.

Use colour and sound (for example, classical music) to raise your energy levels and uplift your moods.

Take a class, and/or read books about psychic development, spiritual growth, and expanded awareness.

If you are in business for yourself, pay close attention to electronic media: Revise your website, and develop connections with people in radio or broadcasting.

Work with the Law of Attraction, as your powers of manifestation are heightened under this vibration.

Affirmation:

I have unlimited potential. I welcome my spiritual growth and greater awareness.

Your 22 Personal Year

Focus: The Vision

If you are in a 22 personal year, your focus will be mainly on the physical and material aspects of life. You will be concerned with strengthening your foundation and building your wealth; however, the requirements of this master number dictate that you must approach these areas with a high degree of consciousness.

You will receive inspiring ideas for personal and professional growth, and practical solutions to situations that may have previously seemed overwhelming. This is a good time to deal with anything that hasn't been satisfactorily resolved within your own personal life, and then move on to helping others. The key here is to think in broad terms, to "dream big" but remain well organized and practical, as you relate everything to "down to Earth" reality.

The 22 year often brings opportunities to make important connections and share expertise with large groups and organizations. Some of these connections may be with individuals or groups outside of your own country.

A Grand Vision and a Larger Audience

My friend, sound therapist Sharon Carne, began her 22 personal year with two momentous events. The first was an unexpected but very rewarding trip to Turkey where she and her husband enjoyed attending their son's wedding and bridging language and cultural differences to build a relationship with their new daughter-in-law's family. The second was the release of her informative and inspiring book, "Listen from the Inside Out"[2] available through her website, www.soundwellness.com.

Midway through her year, Sharon reported that her work had truly gained momentum, that she was spending many working hours refining her vision and

---

2   Carne, Sharon, <u>Listen From the Inside Out</u>, Mountain Rose Music; Calgary AB Canada, 2010

*refocusing her workshops, and that the Universe had
gifted her with many new opportunities.*

You may be required to make some important decisions this year. Although your intuitive abilities will be strong, the 22 calls you to gather factual information, and if necessary consult with various professionals, so that your decisions are based on sound reasoning as well as intuition.

This year doesn't usually indicate career movement, although it will bring increased responsibilities as you work hard to bring big ideas into reality. Because you are receiving so much attention, you may sense a slight "invasion" of your privacy. Be discriminating in terms of sharing privileged information. Operate on a "need to know" basis. Your skills in diplomacy are sometimes put to the test in a 22 personal year, and you may need to re-establish your personal boundaries as you find ways to deal with others in a contentious situation.

Under this vibration of attainment, some of your energy will be directed toward your career, finances, and long term security, and some of it will be extended to altruistic pursuits. As a higher octave of the number 4, the 22 favours building a firm foundation for growth and expansion. As an ancient symbol for the circle, it represents completion and fullness of potential.

The 22 year holds potential for financial gain as long as you don't give in to extravagance. You will manifest material and intrinsic rewards when you integrate spiritual laws and work towards the highest and greatest good.

Important new opportunities generally open up towards the second half of a 22 year, and if you take on a new enterprise it will be with great enthusiasm, vision, and strength of conviction. Your judgement will be very astute, and any decisions that you make in terms of finances should prove to be rewarding.

The 22 personal year often indicates a strong connection with your feminine side, and for young women, this can sometimes indicate pregnancy. It is normally a time of strength and good health. Quiet time for meditation, relaxation, and reading books about metaphysical topics will be essential to your well being, and should be a part of each day. Travel is favoured this year, particularly travel over water.

Congratulations, you have entered a very powerful time in your life!

Proactive Choices for your 22 Personal Year

Focus on your long term security.

Dream big: practice prosperity consciousness and possibility thinking.

Work out details and follow logical progression in your goal setting and action plans.

Take notice of any unnecessary or counterproductive "tolerations" that have held you back. Solutions will become apparent if you give some thought to the situation.

Focus on productivity: consider the ultimate benefits of your effort.

Review your return on investment, not just in terms of your financial investments, but also in terms of your time and effort. Ask "Am I getting what I'm worth?"

Become involved in one or more philanthropic causes, preferably in a leadership capacity.

Keep your energy levels high with good personal health practices.

Re-establish and strengthen your personal boundaries...learn to say "no".

Review past accomplishments and give yourself credit.

Plan a trip, (or expand your business) to someplace that is out of the country.

Affirmation

I work in harmony with Divine inspiration, to create prosperity and peace for myself and others.

Your 33 Personal Year

Focus: Love

It is not common for people to experience a 33 year. This is a number that brings together certain elements of 3, 6, and 9. It brings us a strong sense of purpose and a desire to contribute to the greatest good.

The master number 33 calls for a high degree of authentic personal power and humility. You may be concerned with issues of fairness and justice. Your efforts may be directed toward charity organizations or humanitarian endeavours. You may seek out opportunities to mentor others or work within the education system, much as you would in a 6 year.

The focus will be on contributing your time, energy and resources in a spirit of love and generosity. The primary requirement will be to bring benefit to as many people as possible, including friends and family members, as well as individuals that the Universe has brought to you for a specific reason. The caution here is to avoid any tendency to become overly responsible or to enable poor behaviour in weaker individuals.

Some situations that arise this year may require that you make a sacrifice. In the long run this will bring greater benefit to you and others you care for. Some personal relationships may end this year as family members, friends, and colleagues move on to the next phase of their lives. Much love is required from you, and sometimes the most loving act of all is to let people go. It is also possible that there could be an element of forgiveness involved as certain relationships end.

On a brighter note, this is a year when you will attract new people into your circle. These new associations and friendships will have the potential to bring you deep personal fulfillment. Any existing relationships that are serving your highest good will become closer and more enduring.

Building Professional Relationships

Charlene was getting her coaching career off the ground when she began her 33 personal year. She became very interested in the legal system, and spent some of her time volunteering with the police in their interpretive center. Working with visiting grade six students helped her to hone her communication and leadership skills.

She also stepped up her networking that year and ended up meeting three key people. One of these ladies became a close friend and mentor, while the other two collaborated with Charlene on a coaching project. Although they put considerable time and effort into their project, they were unable to move forward with it and made a difficult decision to let it go. (Two years later the ladies have resumed work and the project is well underway.)

This was not the only thing that Charlene had to let go of in her 33 year. Although her relationship was working well for both her and her fiancé, they ended up having to postpone their wedding for a full year, due to unavoidable complications.

In terms of your career, the master number 33 places you in an advantageous position to call upon innate wisdom and knowledge, to assert your point of view, and to overcome obstacles that arise. You will become increasingly aware of the power of words. You have increased powers of persuasion, and you are in a position to uplift and encourage others through your use of spoken and written language.

The 33 year often gives us reason to be optimistic about our finances. We may need to be careful about spending too much, but on the whole, finances are protected, and often increased.

You will feel the weight of your responsibilities and commitments this year, and will be required to keep a positive attitude and avoid depression, self-pity, or feelings of disempowerment. Be aware of the possibility of mood swings, as the experiences you have this year will be largely in the emotional realm. There will be moments of sorrow, and moments of supreme joy. Your ability to perceive and appreciate beauty is heightened, and whenever you are feeling tired or depleted, you will be able to replenish some of your energy by playing or listening to music, or expressing yourself through some artistic activity.

This year you can be a powerful force for the good of humanity.

Proactive Choices for Your 33 Personal Year

Create a nurturing personal space.

Replenish your life force through natural surroundings.

Take time to enjoy visual and performing arts.

Listen to classical music.

Practice yoga, Tai Chi, or meditation.

Structure quality time with children, parents, or other members of your family.

Seek harmony in your personal relationship issues, and gracefully release those that are not in your best interest.

Avoid over-extending yourself with too many commitments.

Take care of your health needs, with emphasis on rest and nutrition.

Read inspirational books and magazines.

Remember; "It's hard to spread sunshine without getting a little on yourself."

Affirmation:

The Spirit of Love flows through me now.

Connecting With the Energy of Your Personal Year

Now that you have calculated your personal year and become familiar with the influence of that particular number, you may have noticed that some of the choices you have made or actions you have taken recently seem to be congruent with that number. People are usually working instinctively, either on a conscious or subconscious level, with the energy of their year. For example, I often meet clients in a 4 year who tell me that they are currently organizing their home and office, people in a 6 year who are renovating their house, or people in a 7 year who say that they have recently backed out of several commitments so that they can have more time to themselves.

Give some thought to the following reflective questions, or better yet, write about them in your notes. This will help you to gain even more benefit from your personal year. (Remember, you began your personal year on your last birthday. Your personal year changes on your birthday, not with the calendar year.)

How is my personal year going so far?

Are there elements of my personal year that I find encouraging?

Are there elements of my personal year that cause some concern?

Does this vibration support the goals that I am currently working on?

How has it affected my work? My social life? My close relationships? My finances? My personal growth?

In what areas of my life do I experience the greatest sense of accomplishment this year?

Are there areas of my life where I feel more frustrated this year?

What choices have I made or actions have I taken this year that are congruent with the energy of my personal year?

After reading about my personal year, is there any action that I could initiate or thought process that I could change, that would bring greater benefit to my experience of this energy?

Journaling is a powerful tool for self discovery and clarification. Revisiting these questions a couple of times during your year, as well as at the end of your year, can provide you with several "aha" moments, give you a greater sense of direction, help you to put your feelings and your experiences into perspective, and help you to release the past.

At this point I'd like to encourage you to do one of the exercises that my students do in our workshops. Look back over some of the milestones in your life and calculate the personal year that you were in at that time. You'll find it fascinating to see what number was dominant in your life the year you graduated from high school, got married, bought your first home, moved across the country, became a parent, etc.

Notes About My Personal Year

Notes About My Personal Year

Part Three
Know Your
Personal Month

Your Personal Month

Knowing the number of your personal month helps you to choose the right time to begin certain short term projects or to initiate action that moves you forward with major decisions.

What is a Personal Month?

Your personal month is a period of time that adds another layer of energy to the dominant energy of your personal year. The events that occur, the themes that emerge, and the influences that are brought to bear will be similar to the themes, events and influences of the same number personal year; but, of course, they will be of shorter duration and the effects are not usually as far reaching as those of the personal year.

Since this period of time lasts a little over four weeks, you are likely to notice that energy at work in your current situation. Sometimes the number of your personal month facilitates significant movement toward your goals and contributes to positive outcomes. In this case, we say that number *supports and complements* your personal year. We generally find that period of time to be quite comfortable, and we often have a sense of accomplishment by the end of the month.

Sometimes your personal month *provides release* if the year has been tense so far. It may be a month that allows you to regroup and strategize, to regain a sense of balance. For example, if you are currently in a year that is focused mainly on your studies and career matters, your personal month may provide some welcome opportunities to relax or to socialize. If you are in a year that emphasizes responsibilities to others, the personal month may bring you some much needed time to yourself.

A personal month can also *intensify* the energy of your year. Depending on your own unique circumstances, this may mean either added enjoyment, or several unexpected opportunities to practice being patient or strengthening your faith as you deal with stressful situations.

The personal month that begins in September will always intensify the energy of your personal year.

Sometimes the energy of your personal month seems so *opposed* to your personal year that you experience delays, frustrations, or resistance. The Universe definitely has ways of getting our attention, and even protecting us from ourselves. It has ways of telling us to:

o   Slow down

o   Pay attention to the people we love

o   Put our own oxygen mask on first

o   Rethink our plans, or...

o   Stop stalling and get to work

When we have been diligent and honest with ourselves and others, and we are still met with delays and resistance, it's either because we are attempting to do something that is wrong for us, or we are attempting to do something at the wrong time. Trust in Divine Timing, and take it philosophically.

Please note that balance and potential for conflict is highly subjective. Whenever there is potential for conflict, there is also a balancing and correcting influence. As always, the most important factor in the equation is not so much the situation we are dealing with, as it is our own personal reaction.

You will find it helpful to mark your personal month on your calendar and circle the day it begins.

Proactive choices for your personal month will be the same as those for the corresponding personal year.

How to Calculate Your Personal Month

The personal month is found by adding the number of the current calendar month (1 for January, 2 for February, etc.) to the number of your personal year.

Reduce this new sum to either one digit, or if it is a master number leave it as that.

For example, if your personal year is a 7, and you want to know what month you'll begin in July, the calculation will be 7+ 7= 14, 1+4=5.

Although the calculation is quite easy, the table below is easier:

Personal Year	1	2	3	4	5	6	7	8	9	11	22	33
January	2	3	4	5	6	7	8	9	1	3	5	7
February	3	4	5	6	7	8	9	1	11	4	6	8
March	4	5	6	7	8	9	1	11	3	5	7	9
April	5	6	7	8	9	1	11	3	4	6	8	1
May	6	7	8	9	1	11	3	4	5	7	9	11
June	7	8	9	1	11	3	4	5	6	8	1	3
July	8	9	1	11	3	4	5	6	7	9	11	4
August	9	1	11	3	4	5	6	7	8	1	3	5
September	1	11	3	4	5	6	7	8	9	2	4	6
October	11	3	4	5	6	7	8	9	1	3	5	7
November	3	4	5	6	7	8	9	1	2	22	33	8
December	4	5	6	7	8	9	1	2	3	5	7	9

When Does Your Personal Month Begin?

This is where the calculation can get a little tricky. In order to make the most of the energy of each month and each day, it is absolutely essential to know when your personal month begins.

Since my birthday is on the first day of the month, it is always easy for me to know when my personal month begins and ends. My husband's birthday is on the fifteenth day of the month, so his personal month doesn't begin until halfway through the calendar month.

Your personal month begins on your birth day, in other words, the day of the month that you were born.

For example, if your birthday is February 8, then the new vibration for each month of your year will begin on the 8th day of that month, (March 8, April 8, etc.).

If your birthday is August 20, then your new month always begins on the 20th day of the month.

Let's take one more example. This person's birthday is August 30th and on his birthday in 2011 he begins a 6 personal year. Since August is the 8th month, his new month will be 8+6=14, 1+4=5, a 5 month. It will start on the thirtieth day of the calendar month. All through September he will be in a 5 personal month. Then on September 30th he will begin a 6 personal month, (9+6=15, 1+5=6), and on October 30th it will be a 7 personal month, (10+6=16, 1+6=7). His personal month will always start on the last or second last day of the preceding month, and continue until the last or second last day of the next month.

People born on the 31st of any month may find it confusing in the shorter months, April, June, September, and November, just as those born on the 29th, 30th, and 31st will have to adjust their calculations in February.

The best way to handle this is to consider the last day of any of those shorter months as the first day of your new personal month. You will definitely feel the energy shift at that time and making an arbitrary choice like this will help you to keep on track with your personal days.

The Energy of Your Personal Month

Once again, add the number of your personal year to the number of the current calendar month, and reduce to one digit or a master number. Just to make sure, double check with the table on page 57.

The number that you have now will tell you about the type of energy, activities, and possible concerns that will influence your life for a brief period of four to four and a half weeks.

Your 1 Personal Month

A 1 personal month will usually bring renewed focus and fresh perspective. You are likely to feel more energized and more deeply committed to whatever initiatives are underway in your life right now. A personal matter or issue that's been on the back burner for a while may rise to a position of priority. This month you decide to take control of the situation, take the initiative, seek out professional help or rely on your own resources to remove obstacles and get things flowing again. By the end of the month you feel relieved that you have taken action and are moving forward with your plans.

Since 1 is the number of all things new, you may start a project that is related to your personal year. For example you may start a new job or a new position with your current employer. You may begin a fitness program or a home project, or even break ground on a new home that you are building. It is highly likely, in a 1 personal month, (or year), that you will embrace a new opportunity or project with such enthusiasm that you will need to be careful not to burn yourself out in the initial stages.

Another possibility for the 1 month is that you may use this time to roll out a new marketing campaign, workshop, product, service, or creative endeavour that you have been working on behind the scenes for some time. The same applies to a household initiative such as a renovating, decorating, or landscaping project. You may have spent the past several months looking at books and magazines, or choosing colours or materials, and this is the ideal month for the work to begin. The Universe knows, and you will likely find that regardless of whether you arrange it that way or not, somehow this is when the people and resources you need will be available.

If you are single, and looking for someone special to share your life, this will be an ideal month to get out and meet people, or to join a new group, start a course, or take up a new hobby. Quite often new jobs or new positions within your old company will begin in a 1 month.

The energy of the 1 personal month will be strongest if you are also in a 1 personal year. It will also support, complement, and/or intensify the energy and experience of a 3, 5, 7, 8, or 11 personal year. It may bring either balance, or potential for conflict or resistance in a 2, 4, 6, or 9 personal year.

Your 2 Personal Month

This is an excellent month to combine your resources and expertise in the workplace. There can be opportunities to serve on a committee, or to get behind a worthy initiative and show energetic support for one or more colleagues. It's definitely not your turn for the spotlight, but if you enjoy that feeling of intrinsic reward, this month will be a great time for teamwork.

At home, you may be working with your partner or a good friend toward a mutual goal. In both your personal and professional life you will be dealing with details and short term tasks that require your immediate attention. Energy levels are usually lower in a 2 month, and taking care of all those details may cause you to feel overwhelmed for a while. Be careful not to over-promise. If and when you make a promise, do it with every expectation of delivering the goods.

For both men and women, it will be a good time to connect with your feminine side. If you are in a relationship, take time for some special activities with your partner. Quiet dinners and a lovely weekend away (preferably near water) are favoured during this temporary vibration.

Be aware that it may not always be a dreamy, romantic month for you. It might be a time when you will need to be entirely honest with yourself, and confront any relationship issues or other situations that have been diminishing your strength. Sometime during these few weeks, contentious issues could arise, and you may need to assert yourself in a situation with your partner. A spirit of compromise should prevail throughout this month, although it will also be important for you to ensure that you are being treated with respect in all of your relationships.

At some point during a 2 personal month you may be weighing the advantages and disadvantages of a certain course of action, and trying to make a difficult decision. This is not usually a momentous, life-altering decision, although in the case of a personal relationship it can be. The difficulty sometimes lies in our reluctance to come to terms with cold hard facts.

The energy of the 2 personal month will be strongest if you are in a 2 personal year. It will also be strong in an 11 personal year. This month will support, complement, and/or intensify the energy and experience of a 4, 6, or 22 personal year. It may bring balance, in a 3 or 5 personal year, and will likely bring potential for conflict or resistance in a 1, 7, 8, or 9 personal year.

Your 3 Personal Month

Although it can sometimes bring unwelcome news or surprises, the 3 month is usually an optimistic and enjoyable period. If you've been in any kind of a rut, either socially or with your business concerns, you are likely to feel the pace of life picking up again. Even if you're actually in a 4 or 7 personal year, something inside of you says there's been enough cocooning, moping, studying, or working, and you start to kick up your heels. In this case, it can often be like a little reward for staying on course, and a little break from more serious matters.

This month features communication, and involvement with others. You will be both giving and receiving a lot of information by phone or e-mail during these few weeks. Listen well, and make sure that you don't divulge too much information. The challenge for some in a 3 month is to differentiate between fact and fiction, and to maintain focus despite distractions.

You may begin to see early signs of interest in and support for initiatives that you began in previous weeks or months. Particularly in the workplace, the spotlight will shift and your position may become stronger. With an element of heightened personal magnetism, you may be asked to present at a board meeting or possibly to speak at a conference out of town.

The 3 month usually brings opportunities for business networking and socializing. You may decide to add some new pieces to your wardrobe, or change your hairstyle. If your lifestyle and career supports it, this is a good month to meet with an image consultant or public relations specialist.

This month can bring an active social life, as you meet with friends and family members for laughter, fun, and sometimes for celebrations. It's a great month to take a vacation with your partner and/or children. (Have fun, but be careful that you don't overspend.)

It's also a great month to make progress with any creative project that engages your interest. You may want to decorate a room, put some family photos in a scrapbook, or spend more time writing.

The energy of the 3 personal month will be strongest if you are in a 3 personal year. This month will support, complement, and/or intensify the energy and experience of a 5, 9, or 33 personal year. It may bring balance in a 1, 2, 6, or 8 personal year, and will likely bring potential for conflict or resistance in a 4, 7, 11, or 22 personal year.

Your 4 Personal Month

Similar to a 4 personal year, your thoughts will turn to practicalities and matters of personal security this month. This may involve a close examination of your finances and investments, but it is more likely to involve actual material assets, such as your home or vehicle. The focus for the next few weeks could be on a home maintenance issue or a landscaping project. If you happen to be looking for a place to live, this vibration certainly favours reading the rental or real estate ads, viewing properties, and in general taking care of your basic needs.

If your 4 month falls in the spring, it will add extra support to any work that you do in your garden, and would be a favourable time to plant some vegetables or healing herbs.

This will also be an excellent month for you to take care of any matters concerning your physical health. If you have been ill, it's a good time to make appointments and see your health care practitioners. This number supports you as you develop and follow plans for improving your health.

Since the number 4 encourages a work ethic, there will probably be some pressure on you to meet deadlines and produce results, both at work and at home. Do your best to organize your work space and schedule. Be clear about the tasks that are expected of you and systematic in your approach. With the typical constraints of the number 4, your own priorities may be put on the back burner for this period.

Your 4 month may be a 13/4. This will not normally be as expansive or life-altering as a 13 year, but you will probably find that your agenda is very full and there are challenges with scheduling your time. The 13 month will require that you take some time to revise and adjust your plans. Contentious issues may arise, and you will need to be diplomatic but direct in voicing your opinions.

The energy of a 4 personal month will be strongest if you are in a 4 personal year. This month will support, complement, and/or intensify the energy and experience of a 6, 8, or 22 personal year. It may bring balance in a 1, 7, or 9 personal year, and will likely bring potential for conflict or resistance in a 2, 3, 5, 11, or 33 personal year.

Your 5 Personal Month

Whatever your personal year, the energy of the 5 month will bring changes and surprises your way. At least one or two situations are likely to arise that will require some immediate attention. It is possible that some of these situations may seem to move you forward in terms of goal attainment; however, it is also possible that you could meet with some unexpected resistance to your plans and strategies.

There will be a need for you to communicate with others outside your usual circle. For example, if you are in business and concerned with promoting a product line or service, this month may bring more opportunities to connect with your target market and show others what you have to offer. Be aware that it could also bring a few delays with suppliers or product distribution, or with finalizing a contract.

On a personal level, you may be seeing new health care professionals, a new lawyer, accountant, or hair stylist, or you may be dealing with some unexpected family matters. You will need to be out and about and putting your point across to others, either on your own behalf, or else as an advocate for someone in your family.

The energy of the 5 month will support any writing projects that you have underway, and will be especially useful in bringing your persuasive abilities forward if you are writing promotional material. For example, it would be a great month to revise your website or write a proposal for a grant.

One of the more enjoyable elements of a 5 month is that you may have an opportunity to get a little break from ongoing responsibilities. Like the 3 month, it may bring more social activity, and possibly a vacation. In fact, if you are looking ahead and booking a vacation to some part of the world that you have never seen before, your experience will be rich and full if you choose to go in a 5 month. Work to create a balance between taking care of important details like flights and accommodations, and leaving room for spontaneity and synchronistic opportunities.

The energy of a 5 personal month will be strongest if you are in a 5 personal year. This month will support, complement, and/or intensify the energy and experience of a 3, 8, 9, or 11 personal year. It may bring balance in a 1, 4, or 7 personal year, and will likely bring potential for conflict or resistance in a 2, 6, 22, or 33 personal year.

Your 6 Personal Month

Just as your 5 personal month had you thinking about freedom, and wanting to spread your wings, your 6 month will most likely bring a need or at least a desire to remain close to home. There are some reasons that you might travel in a 6 month. These would include traveling to enhance or improve a romantic relationship, or to see family members who are at a distance.

Speaking of family members, there is a possibility that you could be feeling "spread thin" this month. For example, you may be giving time and energy to several different members of your family, or to one individual who is particularly in need of your support right now. (Do make sure that you are not enabling anyone to take advantage of your kindness.) You may also be trying to create a harmonious situation where there has previously been some disagreement.

This month will bring you opportunities to spend time on personal creative endeavours and to move forward with a minor home renovation or a short term decorating project. It will seem that the elusive trades people that you had trouble contacting last month will now be available and at your door.

If you are in the market for new furniture, you will enjoy getting into the stores this month. Similarly, if you are looking for a new home, this is the month to have your house on the market and also to get out there and look for something new. Real estate transactions that are initiated this month will usually have favourable outcomes.

Issues that come to the surface this month sometimes involve dealing with your child's school or with the legal system. Because the 6 brings benevolent and protective influences, you are likely to notice that any project that comes to completion this month or any issue that gets resolved, will either turn out to be completely in your favour, or else will bring an element of compromise that you are able to accept without resentment.

The energy of a 6 personal month will be strongest if you are in a 6 personal year. This month will support, complement, and/or intensify the energy and experience of a 2, 3, 9, or 33 personal year. It may bring balance in a 4, 8, or 22 personal year, and will likely bring potential for conflict or resistance in a 1, 5, 7, or 11 personal year.

Your 7 Personal Month

As you move into this personal month, you may be aware of some unfinished business, or details that require your attention. For example, this might be a good month to pay off an outstanding loan or bill, to cross some distasteful item off your "to do" list, or to finish gathering information that you need before you can move forward with some initiative. Author Juno Jordan refers to the 7 as a number of "mental housecleaning". [3]

In your 7 month there will be reminders of your past coming to the surface. You will be reflecting on the past few months for sure, and assessing your progress. You may also find that other issues, possibly painful memories that you thought had faded completely, will come back under scrutiny as well. At times like this, reflect on how far you've come since the event took place, and remember that the words Lesson and Blessing are almost the same. Give thanks for lessons received and lessons yet to come, blessings received and blessings yet to come.

During this 7 month you are likely to take a close look at one or more areas of your life, (relationships, career, finances, home etc). You will be taking inventory and becoming increasingly mindful of strengths, weaknesses, opportunities, and threats. The 7 temporary vibration will help you to gain a more analytical, philosophical, and perhaps spiritual mindset, so that you are better able to rise above any emotions or ego based fears that might be compromising your peace of mind. For now, it is best to keep your thoughts and plans to yourself.

In terms of your social life, this is likely to be a quieter month. For example you may be recuperating from an illness, some of your friends or family members may be on an extended vacation or business trip; or, after fulfilling duties and taking care of others in your 6 month, you feel ready to withdraw and nurture yourself. It is a perfect month to go on an organized retreat or to create your own retreat at home.

The energy of a 7 personal month will be strongest if you are in a 7 personal year. This month will support, complement, and/or intensify the energy and experience of a 1, 4, or 11 personal year. It may bring balance in a 5, 8, 9, or 22 personal year, and will likely bring potential for conflict or resistance in a 2, 3, 6, or 33 personal year.

---

3   Jordan, Juno, <u>Numerology The Romance in Your Name;</u> DeVorss Publications, Camarillo California, USA; 1965

Your 8 Personal Month

After the relative calm of a 7 personal month, the 8 month brings action and increased momentum. This month offers opportunities and brings its own set of requirements. It can sometimes be a stressful and demanding time. Planning ahead and holding high expectations will help you make the most of this month. Your attention and effort turns to the practical realities of your day to day life, and specifically the larger themes that support your lifestyle, such as career, transportation, shelter, and health.

There are personal business concerns for you to address, which may include the purchase of some big ticket item such as an appliance, a vehicle, some new furniture, or investment property. If you have been planning on making any type of major purchase, this is a good month for you to negotiate prices and put your money down.

The 8 month calls for decisive action. You will be gaining a greater sense of commitment to some major goal or long term vision. You may have increased responsibilities at work, and important decisions to make. Certainly in the 8 month you may see positive developments in your career, developments which are likely to have an impact on your financial status. This may mean that you get an unexpected bonus, or that you receive a promotion and raise. If you are self-employed, the 8 month is a great month for you to talk to people and share some of your big ideas. You may sign an important contract or gain a new client.

This month may also bring contentious issues and opportunities for you to strengthen and re-establish your personal boundaries. If you have been engaged in any legal activities, these issues may be coming to an end next month, and could demand more of your time and energy at this time than they have in previous months. The good news is that in this 8 month, you are in a stronger position. You know what you want, and as long as your concerns are more about fairness for everyone, and more about *what* is right than they are about *who* is right, things will likely work out in your favour.

The energy of an 8 personal month will be strongest if you are in an 8 personal year. This month will support, complement, and/or intensify the energy and experience of a 1, 4, 5, 6 or 22 personal year. It may bring balance in a 2, 3, or 11 personal year, and will likely bring potential for conflict or resistance in a 7, 9, or 33 personal year.

Your 9 Personal Month

Just like a 9 year, this month is about bringing something to completion. It will very often usher in a change. The intensity of the energy this month, and the magnitude of the change will depend largely on what personal year you are in. Naturally, if you are already in a period of accelerated change and growth you will find the 9 month quite intense in many ways.

If things are more balanced in your life, the 9 month will serve as a transition period. For example this might be the last month before you take on a new position within your field and possibly even within your company. It could be the end of a period of several months spent getting your house ready to sell. You may bring a series of medical treatments to completion, or finish up an adult education course. In most cases what comes to an end is something that you had initiated a few months before.

Very often in a 9 month, your intuition is strengthened, particularly with regards to the needs of others. You acknowledge the truth about some situations, reach some conclusions about life in general, and gain greater spiritual insight.

This month brings supportive energy for healing, and would be a good time to schedule surgery or proceed with a course of hypnosis, acupuncture or some other type of holistic therapy. Similarly, it's a good time for you to connect with your own innate healing abilities and reach out to those who can benefit from your kindness. (If you are a practitioner, you will likely notice a higher than usual demand for your services.)

You'll be working hard and may even feel pressured as you try to meet important deadlines and fulfill your obligations. For the time being, your own personal wants and needs, and perhaps the demands of your family or social life, may be of secondary importance to what you feel you must do for others outside your immediate circle.

The energy of a 9 personal month will be strongest if you are in a 9 personal year. This month will support, complement, and/or intensify the energy and experience of a 5, 6, 11, or 33 personal year. It may bring balance in a 1, 3, or 22 personal year, and will likely bring potential for conflict or resistance in a 2, 4, 7 or 8 personal year.

Your 11 Personal Month

Regardless of what personal year you are in, it is likely that there could be rapid and even unexpected developments in your 11 month. Your powers of manifestation are heightened and several areas of your life seem to be moving at an accelerated pace.

You may sense that you are in a position to make significant progress with your own initiatives or a worthy cause that you have taken on. You will have more energy to give to this project, more physical and emotional stamina, more clarity, and greater focus.

You may notice that you are connecting with the right people for the right reason. You are well positioned now to draw attention, support, and possibly even financial assistance. Some of this support may come from unexpected sources, and some of the attention could involve radio or television interviews.

There are times when even the best intentions or the most well-meaning people get off-track and start "going sideways" instead of forward. The outcome in these types of scenarios can be difficult for all concerned. In that case, the 11 month will bring the much needed reality check.

Communication in an 11 month can be sudden and surprising. Just opening your e-mail or answering the phone can be an adventure in itself. Some of the people you talk to or correspond with will be supportive and positive, and if there is anyone with whom you have experienced contentious issues, these matters will come to the surface as well.

This is a month of extremes, a month when the truth will be glaringly evident. Be aware that your nerves may be on edge and you will have heightened sensitivity. Keep up your journal and pay attention to your dreams. Acknowledge and honour your feelings.

Sometimes an 11 month brings an opportunity for travel of an enlightening nature, or for a spiritual retreat. You are likely to meet unique individuals who share your interests.

You will not have an 11 personal month in an 11 personal year. Your 11 personal month will support and intensify the experience of a 1, 2, 3, 5, 7, 8, 9, or 22 personal year. It may bring potential for conflict or resistance in a 4, 6, or 33 year.

Your 22 Personal Month

The 22 personal month occurs very rarely. It will always be in November, and only when you are having an 11 personal year. The ancient Celtic people believed that the month of November was a period of time when the spiritual world was closest to the physical world. Your 22 personal month brings the heightened intuition that we associate with the number 11 month, but you now have the grounding and physical stamina necessary to achieve more with it.

It can be a positive and progressive month if you are hoping to move forward with plans that benefit yourself and others in your life. It is a month that favours giving thought to your goals and strategies, refining and expanding your vision, and taking concrete steps toward goal attainment. Large sums of money may be involved. You will feel motivated to apply due diligence, and when you do, you will be in a position to achieve impressive results.

Expect to be dealing with the public, meeting and serving people, and working hard. Your sense of competence, confidence, and personal power will likely be strengthened with the support of this number.

There will be requirements for concentration and attention to details. Regardless of the personal year, you will be dealing with practical matters and possibly solving problems through your heightened intuition. You are grounded, and focused.

Your skills in diplomacy may be put to the test with this vibration, and you may be involved in some type of negotiation. The overall feeling is usually one of being strong, particularly in terms of spirituality, intellect and emotions. In terms of your physical health, it is a month that favours making progress toward gaining greater strength and well being.

Your 33 Personal Month

This will happen only in a 22 personal year, and only in the month of November.

Your 33 month, just like the 6 month, will likely carry a theme of responsibility and relationships. Family situations may arise that require your input, and to an extent some of these situations may require putting your own interests on the back burner for a while. If you are in a leadership position the personal sacrifices may be for the benefit of your community, your organization, or even your country. You may face a tough or even an unpopular decision, and yet you will do so with conviction because you know that it is for the highest good. The number 33 certainly calls for courage.

Be aware that, with everyone's best interests at heart, you may become overly responsible or inadvertently end up enabling someone else's self-defeating behaviours. There may also be a temptation to criticize others; but if you do, it will make its way through the grapevine and cause grief for everyone. As long as you avoid these pitfalls, your thoughts, words, and deeds will carry influence. By the end of this month you will have spoken and been heard. Most likely you will have played a pivotal role in helping to resolve a difficult situation.

There is a lighter side to 33. There may be a celebration or you may be acknowledged for some contribution that you have made. Your talents are often readily seen by others, and this period will favour any artistic endeavours that you are currently engaged in. It can be an excellent month for aspiring performers, particularly if there is music involved. You have a high level of confidence and there could be auditions as well as photo shoots, and recording sessions. You will be connecting with other people in your field, and will need to make sure that you are prepared to listen well. (That double 3 can sometimes make us more inclined to talk than to listen.)

This month you will need to work at staying grounded. Along with the additional responsibility, there could be a tendency to send your energy out in too many directions. Even though it's a master number, the 33 can sometimes be lacking in the stability that we often see with the number 6.

Connecting With the Energy
of Your Personal Month

Now that you have read about your personal month, you may have noticed that some of the activities or events of the last few weeks have been aligned with the energy of that number.

Remember, you began your personal month on the same day as your birth day, and regardless of how late in the month you have your birth day, that will be the beginning of your personal month.

Give some thought to the following reflective questions, or better yet, write about them in your journal. This will help you to gain even more benefit from your personal month:

How is my personal month going?

What areas of my life seemed to be affected most by this personal month?

Has progress been made toward certain goals?

What is the major theme or issue for this month? (e.g. vacation, celebration, career transition, health etc?)

How does the number of my personal month affect these issues?

Are there elements of this number that seem to cause particular stress?

What elements of this number would I like to see more of?

What choices have I made, or actions have I taken this month that are congruent with the energy of my personal month?

After reading about my personal month, is there any action that I could initiate or thought process that I could change, that would bring greater benefit to my experience of this energy?

How do my plans for next month seem to fit with the new energy?

Notes About My Personal Month

Notes About My Personal Month

Part Four
Make the Most of
Your Personal Day

Your Personal Day

In this section you will find descriptions of each personal day and examples of how these personal days can play out in everyday life. Knowing the number of your day guides you in planning personal and professional activities and interactions so that you achieve the best possible results. It helps you to understand the needs of significant people in your life, to stay in the moment, and to make each day count.

How to Calculate Your Personal Day

You have done the hardest part in calculating your personal year and your personal month. Calculating the personal day will probably be the easiest calculation for you.

Simply take the number of your personal month, and add it to the calendar day. The number you get will need to be reduced to one digit, unless it is an 11, 22, or 33.

For example:

If the date is July 14 and you are in a 7 personal month, your personal day is a 3. (7+14=21, 2+1=3)

If the date is May 8 and you are in a 5 personal month, your personal day is a 4. (5+8=13, 1+3=4)

If the date is June 21 and you are in a 8 personal month, your personal day is 11. (21+8=29, 2+9=11)

How Will You Experience This Number?

Not every aspect or element of the personal day will present itself in that twenty-four hour period. There may be 3 personal days when you are actually alone for most of the day, 7 days when you are surrounded by people, or 8 days when you are on vacation and business is the furthest thing from your mind. When that happens, you will find that in some way the energy of the number of your personal day is coming through. For example, some of your time on a 3 day may be spent quietly on a creative activity, some of the people you meet on a 7 day may seek your assistance with analyzing a troublesome situation, or on an 8 day you may exchange business cards with a fellow tourist, with a view to doing business together at a later date.

Very often the number of your personal day makes itself known through "gut feelings", and intuitive messages about how to arrange your day or spend your time.

In many instances external events in your life will be congruent with the energy of your personal day. (For example, you may receive news about the family on a 6 day or a cheque in the mail on an 8 day etc.).

In addition to your experiences, the personal day will indicate your mindset for that day, your level of openness and interest in events taking place, your preferences, your priorities, how you approach required tasks and interactions, and the best way for you to achieve your objectives, both at the workplace and in your personal life.

There is an infinite number of ways in which the energy of personal days can play out, and an infinite number of possible scenarios. The examples that follow will show you some of the ways in which other people have experienced the numbers on their personal days, and some of the ways in which those numbers are likely to make their appearance in your life on a given personal day. As you become familiar with your Personal Number System, you will see for yourself the many different ways in which numbers appear and the many different ways that you can use them for increased success and productivity.

You will find it helpful to write the number of each personal day on your calendar.

Working With the Proactive Choices

The purpose of this section is to give examples of activities and initiatives that are favoured by, and make the best use of each day's energy. Although some of the suggested activities are items that we can choose to do at a time that suits us best, others deal with common sense items that are in our best interest most of the time. The fact that these items are listed with certain personal days does not mean that we should neglect them at other times; it simply means that on that particular day we have the advantage of greater energetic support for these activities.

Not all proactive choices need to (or can) be followed each time you have a particular day; but by following some of these suggestions, and customizing them to suit your own specific needs, you are likely to notice that:

- the energy of each day's number is flowing

- you have fewer obstacles to overcome

- you feel more in charge of situations and circumstances

- you are seeing better results for your effort

- you are gaining more satisfaction and enjoyment out of life

It's important to remember that your personal day is not about what will *"happen to"* you. It's about what you are able to co-create for yourself and others. We never have to let anything "happen to" us. No matter what personal day we're having, understanding the energy and focus of that number, thinking ahead, taking responsibility, and planning realistically, can help us use the energy of all numbers wisely, and avoid struggling or slipping into a crisis mode. Instead we become empowered and prepared to make the best possible use of our day.

Your 1 Personal Day

The Nature of 1

Do you feel that surge of energy and call to action? This is the number 1. Its element is fire and its planet is the sun. It brings focus and heightened mental energy.

A 1 day can make the difference between feeling depressed and feeling optimistic, feeling under the weather and feeling on top of your game physically, feeling unsure about your decisions and feeling clear in terms of what you want, feeling detached and feeling alive and engaged.

Are there a few loose ends from your last nine day cycle... perhaps some calls to make or errands to run? You will feel greater focus and commitment to those tasks today, and you may even be surprised at how efficiently you deal with them. That's a good thing, because today you want to clear away any unfinished business. It clutters your mind and your schedule, drains your energy, and keeps you from making the most of this new day and this new cycle.

The number 1 calls you to step forward on this first day of your nine day cycle and embrace some new beginning. Of course, we're not talking about the kind of life-altering new beginnings that you would initiate in a 1 personal year; but if one of those comes up, then the 1 day is an ideal time to initiate the bold action that is required.

At work, at home, or possibly within your social circle, the 1 day will bring an opportunity to do something different, begin something new, or infuse an existing project with new energy.

This will also be a day when responsibilities will fall squarely on your shoulders. It's not likely that there will be friends or colleagues around to help you deal with issues that arise, and the truth is, today you are probably glad to know that you are on your own. No input means no compromise on your part, and today you prefer to make your own decisions.

Even if you live or work with someone else, you may spend much of your 1 day alone. You may have the luxury of setting aside a chunk of time for something you really enjoy, such as a solitary walk in the park or a soothing cup of tea and a new book. You may feel relieved that you are able to take care of some task that's been on your list for a while; or you may even find that due to unforeseen circumstances you now have the opportunity to run some errands completely on your own, when you are accustomed to having one or more of your children with you.

A Welcome Break

Diane and her husband adopted a special needs child who, even as a young adolescent, requires constant supervision. Diane home schools, so she rarely spends time without her daughter. She was surprised on a busy 1 day when her husband was able to work at home and give her a well deserved break from her parental duties. She found that her day moved along smoothly and efficiently, and she enjoyed the freedom of running errands and shopping for a special birthday gift on her own.

The 1 day favours self-care. Sometimes instead of the call to action it will bring time to replenish your energy after several full and active days in your previous cycle. If you are going through an adjustment period after an illness or a vacation, your 1 day will help you get back on track.

There may also be an opportunity to be deliciously self-indulgent. Has it been a while since you've been your own best friend? Since you've taken yourself out for lunch or a spa treatment? Have you been saving for a new lens for your camera? Do you need a new outfit for an upcoming social occasion? Get out there and hit the stores today! This is a great day to go shopping for yourself, because you're clear about what you want and you know quality when you see it.

Avoid the Pitfalls

Avoid making impulsive purchases that may cause future stress when the bills come in.

Be careful not to take on too much for one day. Make sure you intend to follow through with anything you begin.

Avoid multi-tasking.

Proactive Choices for Your 1 Day

Begin your day and all of its activities with a positive intention for yourself and others.

Look ahead at your "nine day week" and consider what you would like to accomplish or bring into your life during these nine days.

Prioritize and set some short term goals and workable action plans.

Focus on one thing at a time.

Review your budget, and put some money away just for you.

Speak up and express your opinions and preferences.

Schedule some necessary appointments, especially those that deal with self-care.

Plan some more nutritious meals, or begin a fitness routine.

Set some time aside for yourself.

In the spring, use the 1 day for gardening. This is the perfect day to put seeds or plants into the ground.

Go for a run and see if you can outdo your previous record for timing and distance.

Try something new: a new recipe, a new idea, a new networking or interest group, a new charitable organization.

Step up to a leadership position at work or in your community: chair a meeting or take on a project. (Note if this is a long term project, keep it congruent with your personal month and year.)

Write down any new and innovative ideas. Present them to your boss or partner.

Be ready to meet someone new. If it's not too inconvenient, accept a last minute invitation. The Universe may be arranging for you to meet someone you need to know.

If you are in business for yourself, indulge in some "possibility thinking." This would be an excellent day to speak to a new prospective client, attend a business lunch or networking meeting, tap into your creativity to see what kinds of innovative products or services you can offer, or spend time alone reviewing information about a new opportunity that has come your way.

Begin your vacation. If you are already on vacation when your 1 day comes along, this would be a great day to shop for yourself or do something on your own.

Quite often we're in "high gear" on a 1 day. Make sure you take some time in the evening to quiet things down so that you are able to get to sleep.

End your day with gratitude.

If Your Partner is Having a 1 Day

(Please note: It is the nature of the English language that we must often choose gender- specific pronouns. In this section I have used both "he" and "she"/"him" and "her", and encourage you to substitute the appropriate pronoun for your own personal situation.)

Respect your partner's need for time alone.

Be aware that her mind will likely be on work or competitive activities.

If it feels authentic to you, this is a good time to offer enthusiastic support for new ideas or initiatives that your partner has put forward.

Be aware that your partner will want, and possibly expect to have his own way on some issue. This is not the best day to discuss something that requires compromise on both sides.

Today your partner will want to focus on one thing at a time. It's not a good day to bring out the job jar and ask him to do a few things, or to have a serious discussion about a matter that evokes fairly strong feelings. He may take a stubborn position at this time, and may become defensive if it seems like there is some criticism coming forward.

If Your Child is Having a 1 Day

A very young child is almost always strong willed. On a 1 personal day it may be particularly hard to understand why the world, or at least the family home, is not arranged so that her whims and desires are met to complete satisfaction. Summon your patience and best parenting skills, work to create win–win situations with your child, and avoid or at least minimize power struggles.

Set your child up for success and enhance feelings of confidence, by allowing him to try to do something (age appropriate) by himself.

The 1 day may be hard for a gregarious child to understand. Help your child learn to enjoy spending time alone. Set out a few age-appropriate craft materials, some building blocks, or a nice picture book. If your child is resistant to this set up a kitchen timer, so she knows there will be a limit on the amount of time spent alone with a certain task or project.

Provide young children with opportunities to make choices on a 1 personal day. (These could include choices about food, clothing, or books to read.)

If you have discipline issues or expectations to discuss with a teenager, doing so on his 1 day could result in your teen feeling more resentful or rebellious, and possibly taking impulsive action that would bring about difficult circumstances later on.

If You Are Single

If you are single and looking for a significant other, this would be an excellent day to change your routine or to go out and try something new. Be open to meeting new people or perhaps even joining a new group on your 1 day.

Notes About My 1 Personal Day

Your 2 Personal Day

The Nature of 2

Are you seeking comfort, intimacy, and a sense of belonging today? Are you feeling more sensitive, and possibly a bit tired as your day begins? Are you mulling over the pros and cons of a certain course of action that seemed perfectly logical yesterday? This is the 2 personal day. Its energy is feminine, emotional, and intuitive. The element is water, and there is a strong connection with the moon. (Please keep in mind that most months you will have only one 2 personal day.)

Yesterday you were in the driver's seat, and today it's possible that you would like to climb into the back for a while and let someone else lead the way. You may not feel as energetic, because this vibration is slower. In fact, sometimes on a 2 day, you may feel sleepy, or as though you are operating in a fog. You may have a lot on your mind, feel as though you are making more mistakes than usual, or feel overwhelmed by some task that you haven't yet been able to complete.

Wait! Don't go back to bed because it's a 2 day! For the most part, your interpersonal dynamics can be positive and harmonious today. You will have opportunities to show your support and consideration for others who are close to you. Someone in your life, perhaps your partner, child, friend, or co-worker may approach you, either because they need your assistance, or because they need someone to listen. You are grounded and in touch with your feelings, and your supportive feedback will help others to validate their own feelings.

You may connect with someone today who shows interest and wants to assist you in one of your projects. This person may provide helpful information, or introduce you to someone you need to know. You may receive a report with valuable recommendations from someone in a professional capacity, such as an accountant, business coach, or financial planner. You'll be glad to receive this information, although the details may be somewhat overwhelming.

A 2 day sometimes brings a formal negotiation process with a boss or a client, or a request to join a committee and lend your support to a worthwhile endeavour. It can also bring administrative chores, such as filling in forms, going through files, or gathering supportive documentation for someone or some agency. There may be a decision to make. You are in a mood to compromise, and you feel receptive to other people's points of view, but you may have difficulty being decisive. It's possible that you will share some plans with a trusted advisor today, but you will not feel ready to make them widely known.

Quiet companionship is favoured on this personal day. It will be a time for sharing your feelings with someone close to you. The 2 day often brings opportunities to strengthen your connection with feminine energy. If you are a man this might indicate a date with someone special, or even a good visit with your mother or sister. A woman might make use of this energy to meet girlfriends for lunch, or attend a retreat with a group of ladies.

Feminine Energy and Emotional Release

Kathy attended a summer solstice retreat on a 2 personal day. She found that connecting with the other ladies there was a heart-warming experience. She also felt that she had gained tremendous benefit from the healing and emotional release work done by the group; and sensed that her second chakra was stronger as a result.

Avoid the Pitfalls

You may be tired today, and you will be easily overwhelmed by strong energy. Be mindful of any individual or situation that is draining you.

You may feel touchy or irritable. Take a few moments to breathe, relax, and remember that tomorrow will be a new day.

Do not start something new, especially if it will require major effort and a lengthy period of time.

If your agenda is too full, or your workload is too heavy, you will not feel as though you are handling your responsibilities well.

Be careful that no-one is deceiving you or taking advantage of your kindness. Being considerate does not mean being a doormat.

Be careful that you are reading all the fine print in any agreements you are signing. If possible avoid signing agreements until your 4 or 8 day.

Administrative chores can be tedious. If at all possible try to put them off for a couple of days, until you have the advantage of enhanced concentration and stamina that comes with a 4 day.

Proactive Choices for Your 2 Day

Begin your day and all of its activities with a positive intention for yourself and others.

Plan ahead for your 2 day. Make sure you have groceries in the house, gas in the car or bus fare in your wallet, and that the laundry is done, so that all your necessities are taken care of.

Keep social commitments low key. Call a friend, invite someone over for a visit, or plan a quiet dinner with your partner.

Tune into your emotions and if necessary do some clearing by yourself or with a counsellor. Meditate or write in your journal.

You are highly receptive to the healing benefits of positive energy on a 2 day. Listen to soothing and uplifting music. Watch an uplifting movie. Walk by water, or have a relaxing bubble bath. Nourish your body with good food and drink lots of water.

Plan your work to make maximum use of your energy. If you are feeling bogged down or overwhelmed, take just a few minutes to review and prioritize your "to do" list. See what you can let go of for today or delegate to someone else.

This is a good day to consolidate plans or projects that were previously initiated. Plan to tie up loose ends, flesh out details, (there will be lots of details), and consider the "what if's".

Be a good team member. Listen to other people's ideas, and find ways to give positive feedback to colleagues, friends, or family members.

Take pleasure in supporting or encouraging someone else, and be genuinely pleased for their success. This is the way we show the Universe that we too are ready for success in our own endeavours.

If you are in business for yourself, focus in on specific details related to current initiatives or spend some time reviewing customer satisfaction surveys. Meet with employees, clients, or suppliers, and listen well to understand their point of view.

If you are on vacation on your 2 day, try not to over-plan your day with organized tours or trips to the museum etc. Find some quiet time, preferably near water, to rest and replenish your energy. After all that is what a vacation is meant to do for us.

End your day with gratitude.

If Your Partner is Having a 2 Day

The focus today is on partnerships, so if your partner is happy this will result in a desire to spend quality time with you and share her feelings in a positive, loving way. (If something is upsetting your partner, her temper may be on a short fuse today.) Be tactful, diplomatic, and ready to listen.

Plan some quiet time together even if it's a half hour for a cup of coffee. Your efforts to arrange for a quiet dinner or some other relaxing experience will likely be appreciated.

If you are trying to get your partner to come on board with some idea or course of action that means a lot to you, consider approaching the subject when he is having a 2 day. If your relationship is generally functioning well, your partner will be in a conciliatory mood and willing to listen to your point of view. Just don't ask for a major investment of time and mental/physical energy right now, as he may be tired. Discuss the details and if appropriate, bring out the calendar, and set up a time to take action.

This is a day when relationships can be either harmonious or tense. Certainly discussions and debates of varying degrees of disharmony can arise if the partnership is already precarious.

If Your Child is Having a 2 Day

It's possible that a child may feel easily frustrated with certain tasks or obstacles. He may need your support, encouragement, and willingness to listen today. Be careful not to set the bar too high, and be prepared to deal with the child who says "I can't".

Sharing is a concept that many children need to be taught. Usually once they know how to do it, they enjoy the intrinsic satisfaction of giving. Give your child an opportunity to share with a sibling or playmate, and be sure to praise her positive behaviour.

If you are raising a teenager, this would probably be a good day to have quiet discussions and allow him or her to share some information and express concerns and feelings.

If You Are Single

If you are single and looking for a significant other, the 2 day may present you with an opportunity to get to know someone better. Be aware of any tendency to settle for "good" when you can go for "great". Under the 2 temporary vibration, we can make things difficult by not being honest with ourselves or by justifying behaviours that are not in our best interest.

Notes About My 2 Personal Day

Your 3 Personal Day

The Nature of 3

As you step out the door this morning are you wearing a favourite outfit? Are you thinking about who you're going to see and what items you'll likely be discussing with them?

As evening rolls around are you looking good and feeling lively and full of fun? Is there a sense of anticipation and a desire to spend time with friends?

This is the 3 day, the day you put your best foot forward. It is a day that calls you to blend mental and emotional energy as you interact with others and express your ideas and feelings. It's a great day for promoting yourself, or products and services that you are selling. Its element is fire and its corresponding planet is Jupiter.

This will be a day of activity, communication, and information. Most of the communication that comes your way today will require action on your part, and some of it may elicit emotional response. Some of it may involve your children or pets. Some situations may crop up unexpectedly, either at work or at home, and you may have difficulty scheduling your time. Even if you are normally a punctual person, the 3 energy may make it difficult for you to get to meetings and appointments on time.

Smiles and laughter often come easily on a 3 day. If you are a parent or a grandparent, you may have extra time to play with the children in your life, connect with their child-like perspective, and appreciate the way they see the world. This is the number of the inner child, and as you nurture a child, (or a pet), you are nurturing the child within you.

This day is also likely to bring ideas and enthusiasm for any creative project that you have underway. The scope for creativity is very broad, limited only by your imagination. It can include music, crafts, writing, or home decorating projects. If you are not the kind of person who enjoys artistic pastimes for yourself, the 3 day may simply bring opportunities to appreciate the work of others. One of my clients spent a 3 day with friends at a craft sale. She expressed her delight and enjoyment as she described "hand-made crafts, lovely paintings, and graphite drawings that were amazingly detailed, just beautiful".

Friends...News...Entertainment

Belinda enjoyed socializing on a 3 day recently. She had made plans with some friends to come over for a drink before going out to dinner and the theatre. She not only enjoyed the company, but she also enjoyed hearing news about mutual friends. The play was a comedy, so they all enjoyed the laughs, and as Belinda said, "I love not having to cook."

Once you are familiar with your Personal Number System, you may start to arrange your social gatherings on a 3 day; but, even if you don't consciously use the system, you are likely to find, upon reflection, that there has been an added measure of enjoyment when socializing on a 3 day.

Generally speaking, it's a day when you feel cheerful, positive, engaged, and ready for all kinds of activity. Your personal magnetism is heightened and you attract interest from others. With a positive mindset, this is a day when you are likely to be attracting attention and desirable outcomes. You may even attract money or gifts. You may be inclined to overspend today. You just feel so "gosh-darn" good, and you want to share it with others!

Avoid the Pitfalls

Be aware that 3 is not always about "Happy-Happy Joy-Joy". Communication that you receive on a 3 day is often positive, but sometimes it can be surprising or even alarming. If, in some area of your life, there is a crisis unfolding, more information is likely to come to you on a 3 day.

The phrase "madly off in all directions" can apply to a 3 day. Do be aware that your energy can feel scattered, and you can feel drained at the end of the day, unless you are mindful of how you are using your energy.

Time management can be a challenge on a 3 day. Stick to priority items and avoid getting side-tracked with trivial matters or busy work that drains your energy but doesn't contribute to a sense of accomplishment.

You may feel a bit lazy today. "Lazy" can be good for you, when it's done with intention; but do it at home, not at the workplace. If you slip into down time by "default", then it simply diminishes productivity and wastes your employer's time. Even worse, it wastes your time, and your time is your life.

Guard against a tendency to be critical or impatient, and avoid getting drawn into gossip.

People who wouldn't normally be in your life may be seeking information from you. They may be legitimate, and may even represent some organization or agency that you deal with; however, think carefully about how much information they need to know.

Pay close attention to where you place important papers, documents, or receipts, as they sometimes go astray on a 3 day.

Avoid overspending if you are shopping, especially if you are buying clothes, jewellery, or other personal items.

Whenever possible avoid making serious decisions, especially if they involve spending a lot of money.

Proactive Choices for Your 3 Day

Begin your day and all of its activities with a positive intention for yourself and others.

Indulge in some restorative time away from routines and responsibilities. Whether you are taking a nap, reading a book, or watching a movie, do it with intention so that it works more effectively to recharge your batteries and strengthen your energy for the tasks ahead. This way it brings greater benefit to you, and those around you.

Wear something you like and get out of your house or apartment, even if it's just to run a few errands. (Running errands is not the best way to use the 3 day, but sometimes it can't be avoided.)

Have your photo taken for business or personal use.

If possible, use your 3 day for enjoying some of your favourite recreational activities. Activities that are supported by the 3 energy include meeting friends, watching a funny movie, attending a live concert, mixing business with pleasure, (as in a business golf tournament) or working on a creative project.

Enjoy the company of children or pets.

If you are planning a social gathering, set it up for your own personal 3 day. You will enjoy visiting with all of your guests and your upbeat mood will set the tone for the occasion.

This energy favours communication, so get in touch with a friend. If you can't meet for a visit, try to touch base with a phone call or at least an e-mail.

In all your interactions, think in terms of desired outcomes for you and the others you are with. Be aware if anyone is wasting your time and quickly move on to other people and activities.

Pay close attention to information received through conversation (in person or by phone), and information received through e-mail. Re-read important e-mails or documents, just to make sure you haven't missed anything.

If you are in business for yourself, focus on your marketing today. Meet with a graphic designer, or promote your business by presenting to a group or speaking to individuals about your work.

If you are on vacation when you have your 3 day, plan something fun to do with your children, partner, or friends. If you happen to be on a solo vacation, chat with the local people or join a one day tour. This day also favours taking lots of pictures to share with friends back home.

End your day with gratitude.

If Your Partner is Having a 3 Day

Unless there has been some unexpected development at work, your partner is likely in a good mood, and she may have energy to spare for some interesting and fun activities. This can be difficult, especially if you are having one of those "let's get something done" days, but you can work around it. Suggest that you go for coffee together early in the evening, or that you have dinner later on after the children have gone to bed. Sitting across from each other at a table is highly conducive to good conversation and effective listening.

Your partner may receive an unexpected invitation to socialize after work, or he may want to spend time on a hobby or craft project. This could mean that you will be handling household, and possibly parenting responsibilities on your own. Avoid resentment by arranging for your own share of free time. Playtime is good. It helps us to relax and maintain a positive attitude.

If he wants to go shopping, especially for a big ticket item, this is a good day to look around and gather information. Avoid acting on impulse and make sure that you are both committed to staying within your budget.

If Your Child is Having a 3 Day

Today your child wants to be with friends, and wants to be the center of attention.

It is a perfect day to arrange a play date for a young child, or to have a party if his birthday is coming up.

Also, in keeping with the energy of 3 there may be some ego based flare-ups as children are not inclined to exercise tact or compromise when they are having a 3 day.

Be aware that her attention span will not be long, especially on a 3 day, and you may need to have plenty of activities to keep her busy.

Bring out the paint, crayons, or modeling clay so that your child can spend some time exploring her creativity.

If You Are Single

If you are single and looking for a significant other, this would be a great time to go out to a party. Accept invitations. Wear your favourite outfit and set positive expectations that you are going to have a good time and meet interesting people. You'll be looking good, and will find that conversation and a sense of humour will come easily. Let's face it, the 3 is your day to sparkle!

Notes About My 3 Personal Day

Your 4 Personal Day

The Nature of 4

As you finish your breakfast, or take those last few sips of coffee, are your thoughts turning to your "to-do" list? Are you in the mood to take care of some tasks and errands? Are you thinking that you'd like to make some improvements or to bring a greater sense of order and efficiency to some area of your life?

Whatever is on your mind, you have a strong sense of purpose today. The number 4 brings steady physical energy. Its element is earth, and its corresponding astrological body is Earth.

This is the "anti-procrastination" day. On a 4 day we are looking for order and structure, and we take pleasure in having a feeling of accomplishment. Today calls for patience and concentration. Chances are your "to-do" list may grow before the day is over, but even if it doesn't you are focused on getting things done.

You usually feel on top of your game on a 4 day - in charge, and able to work your plan. It is unlikely that you will have any major interruptions to your day. Once your intentions are set, the energy of 4 will likely guide you on a steady course toward achieving results.

A Well Planned Day

Even though she had slept in, Marie felt focused and productive on her 4 personal day. Despite her late start, she did some house cleaning that she felt had been put off for too long. She also sent her daughter outside to weed some flower beds. After the cleaning she watched a You-Tube video about patching holes in drywall, and organized her plans and materials so that she could do that another day. Later in the afternoon Marie had a few errands to run, as she had volunteered to pick up food for a party that she and her husband were attending that night. The day ended with a pleasant evening outside at her friend's house. In her own words: "I felt very positive today. I had my day laid out and everything went as planned."

This is a good day to either set up some appointments regarding home maintenance or to actually have the work done. I once watched a movie about climbers going to Mount Everest. The narrator was very emphatic about the effort that is spent in establishing a solid, well functioning base camp. I often talk to my clients about how important it is to establish and maintain their "base camp" so that they are then better able to climb their mountain. Think of your 4 day as a "base camp" day.

The 4 energy heightens your ability to concentrate on the task at hand, to develop a system and get into some sort of rhythm with what needs to be done. Generally on a 4 day, we have minimal distractions, and as long as we plan our work and work our plan we end up feeling satisfied with our progress and results.

Base camp can sometimes include the immediate surroundings in your workplace. Because it can be more steady and predictable, the 4 day will often bring fewer interruptions and more time for your own workplace priorities. For example, you may be pleased that you now have an opportunity to do some serious planning for a coming assignment or to organize some files, clear off some items from your "to-do" list, and make some improvements to your systems that will result in more efficient use of your time. You may also get together with some colleagues for a strategic planning session.

If you are employed by someone else, you may hear news today about a new assignment that is being given to you. If you are in business for yourself, you may feel your momentum and motivation increasing. You may feel even more strongly committed to doing whatever it takes to move your business forward. You may make some good contacts today, take on a new assignment, or book an appointment to see a business advisor. Remember the energy of 4 brings steady gains rather than quantum leaps.

When is a 4 Day Not Like a 4 Day?

When you find yourself jumping to answer phone calls and send e-mails, rushing to meet deadlines, adjusting to an unexpected change of plans, re-doing an assignment, or dealing with a short-term crisis. True, you are working, in fact you're working very hard; but what happened to the steady structured progress of your 4 day?

If this particular day seems to have gone off the rails for you, and you're having trouble keeping up with your "instant" agenda, it may be that your 4 actually comes from the number 13. Your 13 day may have an ongoing theme of communication and it can sometimes bring the possibility of being misunderstood. The letters in the word "busy" actually combine to a 13. Stop and take a breath. Definitely plan a little break in your day, even if all you can do is to step outside for five minutes or take a moment to stretch at your desk. By calming yourself down and being careful with what you say to yourself and others, you can rise above this and call back the steady energy of the 4. Above all, do not *expect* a 13 day to be difficult.

Avoid the Pitfalls

You may want to dig in your heels or take a firm position on some issue at home or at work; just be sure that you have all the facts.

Be careful not to work too hard on a 4 day, as it could leave you feeling too tired, and possibly resentful.

Avoid getting so bogged down in tasks and busy work that you lose sight of the big picture and the reason for your efforts.

This is not usually the best day to start a vacation.

Proactive Choices for Your 4 Day

Begin your day and all of its activities with a positive intention for yourself and others.

Plan your day ahead, and set realistic, attainable goals.

The 4 favours taking care of your material assets so it's a good day to clean your house, (or have it cleaned), organize drawers and closets, take the car in for an oil change, or begin, and if possible, complete a repair or maintenance job.

The number 4 often draws our attention to our physical health. It's an excellent day to start a diet or fitness routine. It's also a good day to see your doctor or holistic practitioner, or at least spend some time on the phone making necessary medical appointments.

Go to a farmers' market and buy some delicious produce.

Build something, or prepare food for the freezer. Today you will enjoy seeing tangible results, and it will help you to feel grounded as you work with wood, grains, or other gifts from Mother Earth.

Get grounded by spending some time outside. It's a good day to go for a walk in the woods, or take the dog to the off-leash park. In the spring or summer this is a great day to do some gardening and yard work, and in the fall it is a great day for harvesting vegetables.

Do something wonderful for the environment, such as cleaning up litter in a local park or recycling some household items.

Review current circumstances, and evaluate the way you spend time. Check the calendar, organize and, (if necessary) revise your schedule and commitments for the next few weeks or months.

Make plans for long term security. Take care of your financial assets, check your will or investments, and go over your bank statements.

In the spirit of anti-procrastination, use your 4 day to fill out forms, organize files, answer important e-mails or phone messages, or mail a package or letter that someone has been waiting for.

Take some time to acknowledge your efforts and accomplishments. Review written goals and consider how the work you are doing is moving you forward.

If you are unemployed, or if you are employed but hoping to find something new, this is a good day to work on your resume and send it out. It's also a good day to do a job search on the internet or check with some of the hiring agencies.

If you are in business for yourself, try to make this an office day. Close your door, turn off your phone, and take the opportunity to catch up on some of the work that has been piling up on your desk.

If you are having a 4 day while on vacation, this is a good day to re-organize your suitcase, review your hotel bookings and flight information, and organize receipts from your various purchases.

End your day with gratitude.

If Your Partner is Having a 4 Day

If you are in a relationship and hoping to move toward marriage, this is a day in which your partner may want to make some concrete plans for the future. Be ready to discuss your hopes and dreams, and set some mutual goals.

In the best use of the 4 energy, your partner will want to focus on a job or project that is underway. It's best not to distract her until she's had a good chunk of time to gain a sense of progress and accomplishment; however, depending on the nature of the project she may appreciate your help. Then you can both enjoy a sense of satisfaction.

Your partner has probably been working hard today and it would be good for both of you, and help her to unwind, if you suggest a quiet walk in the park after dinner. If it happens to be a day off, suggest a picnic or hike in the woods.

This is a day that favours mutual goal setting; but it is not a good day to bring up a touchy subject or one that requires compromise.

If Your Child is Having a 4 Day

This is a good day to engage your children in some age appropriate chores around the house, such as helping to clean a room or put laundry away. Be sure to set them up for success and help them to feel a sense of purpose and a sense of accomplishment.

Of course, we don't expect children to do chores one day out of every nine—It doesn't work that way! Hopefully they already have some chores to do; but, as they get a little older there are new ways in which they can contribute to helping the household run more smoothly. The 4 day is a good day to teach them how to do something new. For example young children can learn how to set the table for dinner, and pre-teens can learn how to operate the washer and dryer.

If you have a child in school the 4 day is a good time to talk about school work. Children as well as adults often have trouble giving themselves credit for what they have accomplished. This is a great day to help your children acknowledge their own progress and success.

Children may feel overwhelmed by homework assignments, especially if they have fallen behind. The 4 day is a good day to teach your child some time management skills. Help him to set up a schedule for doing homework, or break down a large assignment into incremental tasks. Talk to him about setting standards for the quality of the work that he produces, and help him to take pride in his best effort. As a school teacher I often talked to the children about putting their heart into their work. I have fond memories of a young boy named Willie who, whenever he handed in an assignment, used to say with firm conviction, "I put my heart into it, Mrs. Mac."

This is also a good day for your children to learn about money and the value of spending wisely and saving some, either in their "piggy bank" or in their own bank account.

Take your child out to spend time in nature, and talk about sound environmental practices. Better yet, arrange for her to participate in some type of environmental activity on a 4 day.

Sometimes, and in certain circumstances, grown-ups have to work all day. Childhood should not be that way, so make sure that your child has some down time and learns about work/life balance.

OK, so maybe it's not a day of fun and adventure, but whenever your child is having a 4 personal day you have a perfect opportunity to help him establish a sense of security and a foundation that will enhance his ability to move forward throughout the rest of his life.

If You Are Single

This would be a good day to go to the gym, or go hiking with a group of people who also enjoy outdoor activities.

Today's energy favours giving some thought to and even making some plans on paper about the kind of relationship you would like to have, the dynamics of that relationship, and the foundation that you would like to build with a future partner. Remember, the number 4 leads us to goal attainment, especially when we do our homework!

Notes About My 4 Personal Day

Your 5 Personal Day

The Nature of 5

Do things feel different today? Is there some excitement and anticipation building, or perhaps even an anxious or uneasy feeling? Are you in the mood to be spontaneous and do something different? Are you feeling frustrated or tired? This is the 5 day and you probably sense it right from the get go. It may start out with an early morning phone call just before your alarm clock is set to ring, or a snarl up in traffic on your way to work.

Or it may be that this is the day you leave for vacation; and, although things are running smoothly there is a definite break in your routine as well as a glorious sense of freedom.

The number 5 brings dynamic physical energy. Its element is air and its planet is Mercury. The 5 day challenges your assumptions, upsets the apple cart, and sometimes leaves you wondering what will happen (or change) next. Whether it's a constant barrage of interruptions to your day and plans gone awry, a single appointment being cancelled or postponed, a new business opportunity, a handful of delightful synchronicities, a change in routines, or just one great big surprise, your 5 day will always bring the unexpected.

This does not always mean that there will be dramatic changes. Sometimes it simply means being somewhere else, or even just doing your work in a different way. Sometimes it adjusts the pattern or changes the focus of your nine day cycle. For example, the 5 day may bring a welcome recreational break in your schedule, a chance to slow things down a little, or spend the day at a conference instead of in the office or classroom. It may be the first day back to work after your vacation, or the first day home after some time away.

A New Approach

Julia, a former teacher who tutors several school children, had to write lesson plans on a 5 day. (This is a great day for writing.) She was feeling tired and chose to stay in her pyjamas. She even decided to do her work in bed, with the TV on. By the end of the afternoon she had written fifteen lesson plans and sent them all to the printer from the comfort of her bed!

The 5 day often brings strength to our ability to manifest, as well as delight in spontaneous actions. Something that you decide to do, - some small risk that you take - may end up creating a chain of synchronistic events and fortuitous meetings with new people who turn out to be "kindred spirits".

It is a day that will draw attention to you, and some of that attention could bring positive results for your career or personal life. You may meet someone new and interesting at a social gathering, or hear of a special opportunity at a business networking event, or you may receive unexpected invitations, orders for a product you are selling, or client bookings.

Since 5 is the number of communication, you may receive a surprise invitation or a call from someone you don't normally hear from. You may learn that someone is ill, that your job is about to end, that you have won a trip, or that a new customer is interested in purchasing your products or service.

Avoid the Pitfalls

It's important to make peace with the energy of 5, to be at ease with the unknown. Not all situations that arise within the 5 temporary vibration will be difficult, and some can bring delightful synchronicities.

Be willing to adjust your plans. Don't "swim upstream". If things aren't flowing for you step back and consider a different approach.

There can be a tendency to feel less ambitious and productive on a 5 day. You may feel tempted to avoid or put off something that you know you need to do. In doing so you run the risk of letting people down when they depend on you, or unnecessarily creating a crisis by procrastinating when you should take action.

Watch that waistline. Temptations will be hard to resist and you may over indulge, especially if you are out socializing.

This is not the right day to initiate a serious discussion with your teenager, partner, co-worker or boss.

If it is of critical importance that you be somewhere at a given time, whether you are flying or driving, make a "plan B" in case something needs to be changed.

Proactive Choices for Your 5 Day

Begin your day and all of its activities with a positive intention for yourself and others.

The 5 is about the fullness of life. Intend for it to be rewarding, and full of opportunities.

Plan ahead for your 5 day: Make sure there are groceries in the house, gas in the car or bus fare in your wallet, and that the laundry is done, so that all your necessities are taken care of.

Stay in the moment. Be ready for anything - have a sense of humour and a philosophical attitude.

It's wonderful when a 5 day coincides with your day off. A strong element of the 5 energy is a need for freedom, and even the most fulfilling work can leave us feeling drained if we don't get some variety. An afternoon, or even an hour away from your responsibilities will help you regain your momentum. If you have the time and the money, treat yourself to a massage or a sensuous spa treatment.

Take care of any writing that must be done, including personal or business letters, articles, books, lesson plans, or invitations. Reply to e-mails and send out information.

If you are a business owner your 5 day is a good day to receive, develop, and act on ideas for marketing and promoting your business. This includes writing copy for ads, and publicising events or special promotions. Attend a networking event. Be out talking to people and making plans.

Begin your vacation (with a spirit of adventure!), or look through travel books and begin planning a vacation.

If you are having a 5 day while on vacation, LUCKY YOU! This can definitely bring some excitement to your trip. It's a great day to go on a sight-seeing tour, speak to other people, enjoy the local cuisine, and above all be flexible in the event that schedules change.

End your day with gratitude.

If Your Partner is Having a 5 Day

Be a good listener, as your partner may have some exciting news to share.

If he is dealing with unpleasant news, try to bring about conversation that will either change the focus to something more positive, or at least open up a dialogue about the desired outcome of the current situation.

Look at travel books together and plan a vacation; or try something outside of your ordinary routines, such as going out for breakfast or having a mid-week picnic in the park for dinner.

If Your Child is Having a 5 Day

Your child will want to communicate today, and anything that you can do to encourage this will have ongoing benefits for both of you.

Children often have difficulty with change. They will exhibit insecurity in different ways, but hopefully as a parent you will find the right things to say and do under the circumstances. It always helps to inform children about a change in plans or circumstances as early as possible. Keeping your tone of voice calm and reassuring, talk to your child about opportunities that arise when plans and circumstances get changed. Honour and validate their feelings, but help them to develop a philosophical approach.

Often the surprises on a 5 day are delightful. Listen and share the joy with your child. Depending on the situation, you may choose to celebrate by going out for an ice cream cone, or having her share the news with grandparents.

If You Are Single

The energy of 5 will often bring new people into our lives. Similar to the 1 day, this will be a good day to connect with a new group and expand your horizons. On a 5 day, a work related social function will often bring opportunities to meet interesting people.

Single people who are not meeting new and interesting prospective partners need to consider changing their routines. Small changes can be just enough to bring a big change, and a 5 day is a perfect day to make one of those small changes.

Notes About My 5 Personal Day

Your 6 Personal Day

The Nature of 6

Are you planning on staying close to home today… possibly doing some cooking or working on a decorating project? Or will today's activities involve a trip to see your parents or other members of your family?

The 6 day brings emotional energy. Its element is earth and its planet is Venus. You will find that your 6 day usually unfolds in a calm, steady, (often pleasant), and predictable manner. Whatever you have planned will often work out to your complete satisfaction, especially if it involves seeing or caring for loved ones.

You may visit, call, or receive calls from parents, siblings, or adult children who live at a distance. You may hear of a birth in your extended family, or be a guest at a baby shower or christening. This day will often enhance your sense of belonging and strengthen your connection with those who mean the most to you.

The energy of 6 favours healing, and dealing with the medical profession. For example, you may spend some time today taking your mother to the doctor's office, taking your son to buy new glasses, or getting some lab work done for yourself.

The 6 energy also favours formal education, and a sense of community. If you have children in school you may volunteer in the classroom or attend parent teacher conferences. Even if you don't have school-age children, you may feel guided to volunteer in your community, especially if it is in support of an educational initiative or some cause that will nurture those who are underprivileged.

If you have not been feeling well and need a wellness day, this may be the day you decide to stay home, rest, nourish your body, and regain your balance. Your pace is slower and you have a sense that the important things are being taken care of. There is usually very little personal drama, although on occasion a 6 day will bring news that raises concerns about the well-being of someone close to you.

If drama does occur on your 6 day, it is more likely to happen in your workplace. You may play a key role in restoring harmony between co-workers, or placating a disgruntled client. Instead of conflict resolution, you may step into a role of mentorship, giving advice to a younger staff member. Another possibility is that you may be involved in negotiating salary and working conditions either for yourself, or for a group that you represent.

Our personal environment often comes to our attention on a 6 day, and you may consider some decorating options or make plans to create a new use for a certain room in your house. As an extension of this, the 6 energy sometimes directs our thoughts to matters of real estate and personal property. Since this number is also associated with the legal system, you may find that you are dealing with lawyers or reviewing your will.

Real Estate and Diplomacy

Megan had been concerned about a structure that her neighbour was building on his property, and that she felt might devalue her own property. She used some time on her 6 day to make enquiries at city hall and find out if there were by-laws in place that would protect her. She then went over to share her feelings, "diplomatically" with her neighbour. Megan also met with a realtor that same day.

Avoid the Pitfalls

It may seem that your tasks on a 6 day reflect other peoples' priorities more than your own. You may feel a sense of urgency about meeting your commitments and living up to other peoples' expectations.

Your assistance may be required by several family members or close friends. There may be 6 days when you feel "spread thin".

Be careful about taking on too many commitments. Whatever you take on you must complete, and if there is too much you can end up feeling exhausted and depleted, if not resentful.

Watch the mind chatter, the messages that you are giving to yourself or the sound bites that you are playing in your mind. Be aware of a tendency to worry, or feel depressed on a 6 day, and take positive steps to deal with it. One very effective way is to think about desired outcomes and best case scenarios for yourself and others.

Proactive Choices for Your 6 Day

Begin your day and all of its activities with a positive intention for yourself and others.

Work on an artistic or creative project.

Write thank you notes.

Call or visit family members, for a friendly, newsy chat.

Take a look at family birthdays that are coming up. Purchase and/or mail birthday cards or gifts.

Volunteer in your child's school or meet with his teacher.

Attend a play or concert.

See a healing practitioner. If you are a practitioner, meet with clients or do some distance healing work.

Eat well today. Plan menus, shop for groceries. Cook a delicious and nutritious meal for family members or close friends. (Make plenty of leftovers to stock up your freezer.)

Look through decorating books, or shop for items for your home. (Allow plenty of time for this, as it may not be easy to make decisions today.) Hang pictures or rearrange furniture.

If you are in business, work on building mutually supportive relationships. Call clients and prospective clients to touch base and strengthen your connection, or meet with a fellow entrepreneur to discuss a joint venture.

If you are having a 6 day while on vacation, this energy would favour an artistic focus to your trip...plays in London, art galleries in Montreal etc. It would also be a perfect day to call home or write post-cards.

End your day with gratitude. (In numerology, the letters in the word gratitude combine to a 6.)

If Your Partner is Having a 6 Day

Similar to the 2 day, the 6 offers favourable energy for communication and harmony between partners. If there are any potentially difficult issues arising in your relationship, this would be a good day to be open and honest about them. Since this energy favours compromise and diplomacy, your partner is likely to be willing to work on a solution and come to a mutually beneficial agreement.

It would be a good day or evening to spend quality time together, and if there are children, it would also be a good day for a family outing.

If it works into your schedule, your partner might appreciate you hosting her parents or family members for dinner, or going with her to see relatives.

This would be a great time to discuss and move forward with any plans that you have to make improvements and add value to your home. For example you may go looking at floor coverings together, or work on a DIY project.

If you have wanted to bring up the subject of moving to another house, your partner could be receptive to that type of discussion today.

If Your Child is Having a 6 Day

This is an excellent day to teach your child about the importance of the family unit and the rewards of taking on age appropriate responsibilities.

If he's old enough ask him to look after a younger sibling for a short period of time, or take the dog for a walk. This not only promotes a sense of responsibility, it enhances your child's ability to nurture others.

Have him help out with some household chores today in return for some time spent having fun with friends.

Do something with your child today, perhaps an art or cooking activity.

Engage your child in a family board game or go out as a family for a bike ride.

The 6 day is a great day for children to strengthen their sense of belonging by connecting with grandparents and other extended family members. Even if the family members are at a distance you could arrange a phone visit, or help your child write a letter, or draw a picture for them.

Spend time together looking at photographs of family members, celebrations, or vacations.

If your child is a teenager, encourage communication and sharing of feelings. Discuss positive ways to handle emotions. Help him to see that our true friends are those who validate us and make us feel good about ourselves.

If You Are Single

This is the relationship day.

If you are single and looking for a significant other, this would be an excellent day to do something in your home that would help you create the right environment for a positive loving relationship. Feng Shui books are often full of ideas that are easy to implement into your personal space. This is a great day to take action!

It would also be a good day to have a small group of friends over for a dinner party. Expanding your network of friends and strengthening the friendships that you already have are effective ways to move toward a romantic relationship.

Notes About My 6 Personal Day

Your 7 Personal Day

The Nature of 7

As you begin this day are you thinking about, (perhaps even longing for), quiet moments to yourself? Is there a book that you've been waiting to get into, a project that requires your undivided attention, some "loose ends" to tie up, or some information that you need to gather?

This is your spiritual/intuitive 7 day. Its element is water and its planet is Neptune. Often on a 7 day we spend a significant period of time on our own. Even in your workplace, or in your busy home life, the 7 personal day usually provides a window of time to yourself. After all, the seventh day is meant to be a day of rest.

Your responsibilities are not about to disappear or be dramatically decreased; but, the 7 personal day will often bring a break in your hectic pace. Chances are, there won't be as much e-mail today and the phone will not ring as often. Any communication that does come your way will not require immediate action on your part. Phone calls and other conversations will be short and to the point, and you will likely put off making decisions. Your inner guidance will caution you to be guarded when stating your opinion, even though others may be seeking your input today. (You'll probably tell them that you want to think about it for a while and get back to them in a couple of days.)

This is a number that calls upon us to be organized and ordered in the way we approach our work and run our household. You may feel that you can no longer tolerate a certain pile of papers that needs to be filed, a "scary" kitchen drawer that hasn't made any sense for the past three months, or a laundry hamper that seems to have been overflowing for the past few days. Patience is not your strong suit on a 7 day, at least not for unfinished business, or "tolerations" that have been quietly draining your energy for a while. On your 7 day you will want to attend to such matters, and will most likely have the time and space that you need.

Yes, things will get done today, and this will seem to happen without the effort or possibly the struggle that is required on other days in your nine day "week". Anything that has been previously set in motion will move along at its own pace and come to a satisfactory culmination. The 7 is a great day to "tie up loose ends". Any obstacles that arise need to be accepted philosophically, since constraints and delays that occur on a 7 day are always there to serve your best interest. The key word for the number 7 is "allow".

Your intuition will be strong today, as will your ability to discover gems of wisdom or to probe past illusion and appearances, and discover the truth of certain situations. (Your guides and angels are speaking to you.) On such an introspective day that could mean coming to a certain realization about a logical course of action that you need to follow, or a self-limiting behaviour that you want to overcome. The 7 day shows us how to take the path of least resistance.

The intuitive mental energy of the 7 will help you connect with Spirit, whether you are at work or at home. This is a day when you can truly connect with your surroundings. If you are fortunate enough to be in a natural setting - possibly away from your workplace or your current responsibilities - you will savour the quality time to yourself, and the entire day will bring serenity and a quiet reassurance that life is good.

Spirituality and Restorative Rest

One glorious 7 day, Helen left the city behind to spend some time alone at her sister's condo in the Canadian Rockies. She felt the tension release and her spirits began to soar as she drove west toward the mountains. In the days preceding her trip she had been receiving intuitive reminders about "going with the flow" and releasing resistance. As she browsed through the merchandise at a spiritual shop, she drew a card with the simple message "allow". She appreciated the message and reflected on what that would mean for her, and how she could feel more "in the flow" on a daily basis. Later that day Helen indulged in a refreshing steam bath and sauna and reported that "the evening was capped off with candlelight and reading a good book while listening to smooth jazz".

Avoid the Pitfalls

Whenever possible, avoid entertaining in your home when either you or your partner are having a 7 personal day. The only exception to this would be if you were hosting a gathering of like minded individuals who come to discuss more spiritual or intellectual interests, for example a spiritual book study group.

This is not a good day to shop, and very often things that you buy on a 7 day, especially if they are "big ticket" items, will have to go back to the store.

Do not hang pictures or take on a home decorating project.

Do not go for a job interview. It will be harder on a 7 day for you to "open up" and make a good impression.

For the most part, this day does not favour communications. Making business or personal phone calls, sending out newsletters or other types of e-mail can be tricky on a 7 day. You may end up feeling as though you are trying to wade through mud.

Proactive Choices for Your 7 Day

Begin your day and all of its activities with a positive intention for yourself and others.

If it's not a workday, sleep in or have a little nap.

Schedule time alone for meditation and introspection. Do some writing about a situation at home or at work that has been compromising your peace of mind. As you work in your journal, some insights and truths will be presented to you.

Check into your financial situation, bring your cheque book up to date, pay some bills on line, or pay off an outstanding debt.

Connect with your spiritual side. You could attend a church service, visit a metaphysical book store, or have a reading from a reputable psychic.

Broaden your intellectual horizons by visiting a library or a museum, attending a lecture, watching a documentary film, or studying an area of personal interest.

If you are a student, use this time to catch up on a research project, or study for exams.

Do research and gather information that will help you make a decision. For example, read about the candidates in an upcoming election, or check consumer reports on a vehicle you're thinking of buying.

If you are currently in the process of making an important decision, this will be a good day for you to get out the pens and paper and do an analysis of potential benefits vs. trade-offs. Consider a course of action and write up a list of pros and cons, or do a SWOT (Strengths, Weaknesses, Opportunities and Threats) analysis.

Search for a personal belonging or a file or document that has gone missing.

It's always best to operate on a "need to know" basis. Especially on a 7 day, be mindful of the importance of maintaining confidentiality.

If you are a business owner, this is a great day to review your business plan and do a SWOT analysis of your current situation, or to do some strategic planning with one or two trustworthy advisors.

If you are on vacation and having a 7 day, you might want to spend some time learning about the history of the area you are visiting.

End your day with gratitude.

If Your Partner is Having a 7 Day

Your partner may be feeling tired today, so it's best to avoid shopping trips or big social events, If you do go out, agree before you go on a satisfactory time to come home. If you know you will want to stay later, make arrangements for someone else to bring you home.

Even when there are young children in the house, try to arrange for your partner to have some space and time to herself. Make an agreement that you will take the children out for a little while and ask her to do the same for you on your next 1 or 7 day.

It's excellent for children to see that everyone benefits from time alone. It helps them to develop some positive habits of their own. I remember one occasion when my daughter, Caitlin, was five years old. It had been a demanding day at school and as we were finishing dinner, she said to me, "Mommy, you just need some time alone, like about a hundred years"!

The 7 is a number of order. Avoid projects that would bring about disruption to household routines. This can cause a great deal of stress for anyone having a 7 day.

If Your Child is Having a 7 Day

Allow him to try some age appropriate task by himself.

Show her some games that she can play by herself, or other ways to enjoy time alone.

Take her to a museum, and talk to her about historical events, or the way people lived years ago.

Look at some old pictures together.

Talk to your child about "gut feelings" and intuition. Help him to learn to trust those feelings.

For teenagers and younger children as well, the 7 is a good day to take an objective look at problems and unsatisfactory elements in their lives, and to weigh the pros and cons of possible options.

If you have a teenager, this would be a good day to study or work on a school project. Ask him to show you what is being done, and ask questions about the content of the material being covered.

If You Are Single

If you are single and looking for a significant other, this is simply not the day to do it!

This is a perfect day for you to enjoy your own company, to be alone without being lonely, and to fill your mind with some helpful and inspiring new information.

Notes About My 7 Personal Day

Your 8 Personal Day

The Nature of 8

Ever had one of those days when you felt like you were running from morning to night? A lot on your to-do list? Situations demanding your attention? People you must speak to and meetings to attend? Money to spend? Decisions to make?

Of course we all have days like that and some will say that every day is like that; however, on an 8 day there is often an even greater sense of responsibility. Your words and deeds carry influence, and it seems that others depend on you and look to you for answers.

The 8 represents mental energy and it often brings forward a competitive spirit. Its element is Earth and its astrological body is the great taskmaster, Saturn. It is a number that calls for both common sense and vision.

You may feel quite impatient on an 8 day. You are keenly aware of how your time is being spent and have very little tolerance for any individual or situation that keeps you from taking care of business or getting to your destination.

Most people step up to the demands of an 8 day with a feeling of strength and confidence in their ability to make substantial progress toward larger goals, to take charge of their life and for that matter, their family or co-workers immediate circumstances as well. This can be a rewarding and productive day.

Today you may receive information about a promotion or a competition. If you are an athlete you may feel even more motivated than usual to rise to a certain challenge or establish a new "personal best". If you are in business for yourself, you may receive news about what a competitor is doing. If you are in the corporate sector you may be keenly aware of a need to shine brighter than others in your office if you want to move to the next rung on your ladder.

Remember that 8 is the number of fairness and good judgement. You may be called upon to make an executive decision that will affect others and possibly have long-term implications for their well-being. Contentious issues may arise. You may feel the need to take the upper hand in a crisis or a dispute, or speak to someone who is creating resistance and diminishing the efforts and potential results of the entire group. This may be at work or within your family.

You are in a leadership position today, and you must be on top of your game. You may be required to take decisive action that will affect not just you but those around you as well. Not everything you do will carry long term implications; but on an 8 day you will often have the opportunity to alleviate concerns and implement solutions to immediate problems.

Rising to the Occasion

Anna is a successful business woman who is also Acting Director for her condo board. I met up with her at the end of an 8 day, as we were both arriving at a business women's meeting that she hosts once a month. She was running a bit late, and explained that a water main had broken at her building. The company that manages the building was not working that day, and had no-one on call. Anna herself had been required to step up and make executive decisions as to how to deal with this emergency. She had even been forced to call the police to come and break into a unit that had been flooded.

This day will invariably bring money, decisions about money, or news about money; and, most of the time it will be about money that is coming in rather than going out. For example you may receive a cheque, bank statement, or investment report in the mail. You may take on a new client, or receive a new work assignment that will bring additional income.

If you happen to be on vacation on an 8 day, the energy of 8 will manifest in a different way. For example, if you are in a high level position, you may get a call from the office because they simply can't proceed at this point in time without some input from you; or, if you are self-employed, you may meet someone on the golf course today who is interested in doing business with you.

Even if work is the furthest thing from your mind, the expansive 8 energy may simply come to you as an opportunity to live in the moment, savour the good life, and appreciate the rich experiences that you have co-created through your diligence and positive expectations.

Avoid the Pitfalls

Be careful not to carry a grudge or try to exert influence just for ego gratification.

Be open to other points of view. You create bad energy and resentment if you impose your choices on others against their will.

Promises, promises! Be wary of making promises. You must be able to fulfill them.

Definitely do whatever needs to be done, but avoid getting bogged down with small tasks and busy work.

Although this day can favour business travel, it is usually best not to begin a vacation on an 8 day.

Manage your time and your energy wisely to avoid feeling drained at the end of the day.

Proactive Choices for Your 8 Day

Begin your day and all of its activities with a positive intention for yourself and others.

This is a take charge day. Be ambitious as you plan your activities and meet your requirements.

Submit resumes, go for a job interview, ask for a raise or apply for a promotion.

Take charge of a financial situation today. Meet with your financial advisor, or deposit money into your savings account.

This can be a good day to make a major purchase. On an 8 day you are a discriminating buyer, and it is obvious that you expect the best in terms of product and service.

This is a day for big picture thinking. Devote your time and energy to endeavours that will bring positive, far reaching results.

Attend a large networking or charity event.

Meet or initiate contact with someone in an influential position.

Spend some time going over your plans for this month, this quarter, this year, with a view to progress that you would like to make and wealth that you intend to accumulate.

Deal with difficult or adversarial situations at home or at work. Speak your mind. Be direct, honest, and forthright. The 8 energy calls you to be fair but firm. You will likely gain support from others this way.

If you are a business owner, try to arrange important meetings or presentations on an 8 day, especially if they deal with signing contracts, or raising investment capital.

In you are having an 8 day while on vacation, live in the moment and resist the urge to call the office. Visualize many more exciting vacations in the future.

End your day with gratitude

If Your Partner is Having an 8 Day

Your partner has probably had a demanding day at work, so be aware that it may not be a particularly romantic evening. You might suggest a late day golf game, or meeting at the gym and going out for a healthy meal after your workout.

She may be developing a vision for some project that will require focus and determination. Invite her to share her long term goals and vision with you, and be a good cheerleader.

This is an excellent day to review your financial situation as a couple, discuss your investments and make plans for future increase. Your romantic partnership needs to be a business partnership too, and when either one of you is in an 8 day it's a good time to take care of business.

If Your Child is Having an 8 Day

This day favours lessons in money management, and in developing a sense of prosperity consciousness. Encourage her to save some money for something bigger than a week's allowance can provide.

Encourage her to see the big picture, to make some ambitious plans for the future, and set some long and short term goals.

Facilitate and encourage your child to participate in some sports or exercise. Today she will have quite a bit of energy that will need to be channelled.

It's also likely that your child will be in a competitive mood. There is nothing wrong with trying to outdo your competitor in a sports event, as long as it is done with fairness. Fairness is an important element of this number, and the 8 day provides opportunities for children to learn about this.

It's also good for children to try to compete with themselves, to have a sense of striving for improvement. Again, bring up the idea of "personal best" in age-appropriate ways.

Sometimes parents have no choice about when certain issues need to be addressed; however, if you can, avoid power struggles when your teenager is having an 8 day. It's not a good day for a discussion about problems at school or chores that need to be attended to at home.

If You Are Single

If you are single and looking for a significant other, this would be an excellent day to go with some friends or business associates to a major event where there are a lot of people.

In fact, if there is an opportunity to volunteer at some corporate sponsored charity event that would be a great way to do something for others while meeting new people and making good use of your personal day energy.

Notes About My 8 Personal Day

Your 9 Personal Day

The Nature of 9

Does it feel like you're in a hurry today? Do you have a strong desire to finish something? Are you thinking about all the different hats you're going to wear as so many of your various roles and responsibilities seem to converge all in one day?

You may amaze yourself at how much you are able to get done today. There is also a possibility that you could be feeling extra sensitive, or at least a little tired. After all it is the end of your "week".

This is your intuitive/emotional 9 day. Its element is fire and its planet is Mars. Even in one day, the energy of 9 can bring a variety of people, experiences, and emotions your way. There can sometimes be a sense of loss on a 9 day. It may be the day you hear some sad news about someone in your family, the day you put your pet down, end a relationship, or leave a familiar workplace for something unknown.

There may be a travel theme, such as the end of a vacation, meeting people from an entirely different part of the world, or sending e-mail/talking on the phone with someone at a distant location.

Sometimes on a 9 day we see the culmination of something we've been looking forward to for a while, possibly a social function or a public event that we've been planning. You may finish a creative project or a short term assignment that you took on at work a few days or even a few weeks ago. When a project ends on a 9 day there is most often a sense of satisfaction and a feeling of accomplishment.

This may be the day that the Universe helps you release some item that you no longer wish to keep. For example if your house has been listed for a period of time, or you have been trying to sell your car, it is possible that your 9 day will bring an end to successful negotiations, so that you feel free to move on.

Letting Go

Sue was in the process of moving, selling off some furniture, and letting go of a volunteer position as a host at a community radio station. In addition to this, she worked full time delivering mail. All of this seemed to converge on a recent 9 day.

She reported receiving numerous calls throughout her workday from people who were going to pick up some of the household items that she no longer needed. She made plans to take anything that was left to charity after work, although she encountered a lengthy delay while waiting for her previous landlords to meet her at her old house. After taking care of her moving details, Sue went to the radio station to record her last show.

On a 9 day you may finally get in touch with someone you've been trying to reach for several days, or you may receive a gift from someone. Sometimes this is "merit karma" bringing your kindness and good deeds back to you.

The 9 calls us to show compassion and understanding, to fulfill promises that we have made, and to complete the circle of giving and receiving. We have a deep desire to feel truly connected. The emotions that come to the surface often include love and concern for other peoples' well being. We want to be of service on a 9 day and often feel guided to put our own priorities and projects on a "back burner".

It may be a day when one of our neighbours or friends needs immediate assistance, or a day that we had planned to do something else but one of our children has a medical emergency or an emotional dilemma. Pleasure and satisfaction comes from doing something with and for someone else, and nothing feels better on a 9 day than knowing that we've made a difference.

Your 9 day brings current situations and responsibilities sharply into focus and deepens your motivation, while at the same time it presents challenges in terms of scheduling your time. You may have strong concerns about how to fit everything in... you wonder how you're going to get back to the office in time for that important teleconference after meeting with an important client at the other end of the city... how you're going to get home in time for dinner so that you can take your son to that important soccer game... how late you will have to stay up after the game to put the finishing touches on that important proposal so that you can present it at an important meeting first thing tomorrow morning. Do you sense a theme here? Everything seems important on a 9 day!

Your intuitive powers are strong, but whether you access them or not depends on how well you are able to focus and avoid multi-tasking. If you meditate regularly you may sense that you are going deeper into your subconscious on a 9 day.

This personal day favours both giving and receiving healing on all levels. It calls us to look around and contemplate the deeper meaning of our relationships with others, to appreciate the beauty of life, and the beauty in our surroundings.

Avoid the Pitfalls

As with the 6 day, you may feel "spread thin". When looking at your agenda for the day, use the word "full" not "busy".

Accept interruptions and changes in your plans with a philosophical attitude. Remember that tomorrow your 1 day will bring plenty of support for getting back on track with your own priorities.

Avoid getting caught up in stressful situations. Take a moment to do some deep breathing, stretches, or shoulder rolls. If possible play some soothing music in the background while you work.

Avoid social interactions with people who are not respectful of your personal boundaries.

If at all possible, don't begin anything new today.

Proactive Choices for Your 9 Day

Begin your day and all of its activities with a positive intention for yourself and others.

Plan ahead for your 9 day: Make sure there are groceries in the house, gas in the car or bus fare in your wallet, and that the laundry is done, so that all your necessities are taken care of.

Prepare to be out and about, connecting with others, including people you don't know. Give thought to what you hope others will receive in their interactions with you.

Make an effort to call someone you've been trying to contact for a few days, or reply to some old e-mails and clear out your in-box.

Buy or give a gift, make a charitable donation, or spend some of your time as a volunteer.

Go for a medical check-up or see a holistic practitioner.

Bring a project to completion, or finalize plans so that you can begin the actual work on your 1 day.

Remove unneeded items from your closets and cupboards and take them to an organization that can make good use of them.

Take inventory of your accomplishments at home or at work.

If you are a business owner, this would be a good day to touch base with customers or employees at a distance, or send thank you letters to clients and suppliers who have been supportive.

If you are on vacation, go off the beaten path, and learn more about the people and how they live in this area. This is also a good day to leave for home if your vacation time is nearly over.

End your day with gratitude.

If Your Partner is Having a 9 Day

She will probably come home from work feeling tired today, and will really appreciate it if you look after dinner... especially if you serve her favourite "comfort" food.

If you normally have music playing at home, this would be a good day to opt for the "easy listening" pieces.

Be a good listener on your partner's 9 day. He may have some interesting things to tell you.

Be prepared to take an interest in, and possibly volunteer some time if there is an out of office project that your partner is working on. On a 9 day he will truly value your support.

Be understanding if your partner doesn't seem to have time to focus on you or the home and immediate family. This is not the best day for a romantic dinner, or a private discussion.

If Your Child is Having a 9 Day

Today is a day to expand your child's heart and his horizons.

Share some library books or watch a movie about children growing up in a distant country and culture.

Draw attention to the fact that many children around the world, (and even in their own community), do not have the same number of toys and the privileged lifestyle that children here often take for granted.

This is a great day to take your child to a charity event, or to help him choose presents for less fortunate children.

Help her clean out her closet and select toys, books, or clothing that she would feel good about giving to someone less fortunate.

If you are in any way open to complimentary healing therapies, this would be a good day to take your child to a healer, or just talk to him in age appropriate ways, about the power of our thoughts and the way energy works for us.

If You Are Single

If you are single and looking for a new relationship, this is a good day to volunteer for a not-for-profit organization. You may not meet any one individual who will be significant in your life, but you will be further enhancing your ability to connect with others. Someone you meet on a 9 day could provide further opportunities to meet other people at a later date.

Notes About My 9 Personal Day

Your 11 Personal Day

The Nature of 11

Are you strongly aware of other peoples' feelings today? Are you feeling irritable and sensitive, or angry with someone or some situation?

Did you have vivid dreams and upon waking feel connected with someone in spirit? Do you have an inexplicable feeling that you need to call a certain friend or family member?

Have you just heard that a radio host wants to interview you about your latest project, or a that a potential employer/ major client wants to speak to you?

This is your 11 day. Its element is fire, its planet is Uranus, and its energy is spiritual/intuitive. It is a number of peaks and valleys, a number of extremes.

The 11 often brings jolts of reality, unexpected developments, or sudden news. You may hear something you'd prefer not to hear on an 11 day, but if you do it will be something you need to know. You may hear good news, and find that certain developments, though unexpected, are working out decidedly in your favour.

In keeping with the theme of communication, you may receive a phone call or e-mail from someone you hadn't heard from in years, a real "blast from the past", or you may find yourself caught up in a contentious issue at work or at home. Even though nobody likes to deal with inharmonious situations and interactions, the mental energy of 11 heightens your ability to focus, and to clearly articulate your position while meeting these issues head-on. Like the 1 and the 8, the 11 is a "don't mess with me" number!

This is a number of manifestation. It's possible that today something you have been trying to attract into your life will come out of the realm of your thoughts and into your reality. The saying "be careful what you wish for" can be particularly apt on an 11 day.

If you are out in public, your profile is heightened and you are sure to be making an impression on others. You could have a great opportunity to step into the spotlight, to promote your products or services, a project you believe in, or a worthy charitable cause.

You may have a powerful psychic experience on an 11 day, connecting with angels, spirit guides, or deceased loved ones. You may have a new sense of clarity about some current situation in your life, a realization of truth that for some reason you hadn't been able to see before. This could seem like a blinding flash of the obvious, or a sudden deep conviction that a certain course of action must be followed.

Travel on an 11 Day

In the fall of 2009 I flew to Ottawa to visit my son and present a workshop. I try to avoid flying on an 11 personal day but this time it seemed to be the best option in terms of fitting in with my schedule. I was not at all alarmed or concerned for my safety, but I did feel that there were some surprises in store, and chose to hold the expectation that these would be good surprises.

First of all, the plane was about forty minutes late leaving that day. Four and a half hours later we were making our descent into Ottawa when it suddenly started to angle upward again. Even the flight attendant, sitting in her seat at the front of the plane, looked totally surprised. A few minutes later the pilot announced that Ottawa airport was inaccessible due to heavy fog, and that we would all be going on to Montreal. My first thought was that we might stay overnight in Montreal and I hadn't been there in years.

As it happened we waited on the ground for about three hours in Montreal, before heading to Toronto where we were given hotel and meal vouchers. In a situation like that people start talking to each other, and I love opportunities to get to know people! I joyfully and completely surrendered to the situation, viewing the whole experience as a delightful synchronicity. By the time we arrived in Ottawa the next morning, I had enjoyed the company of several fellow passengers, one of whom came to my seminar in Ottawa the following weekend, and one of whom booked a reading with me when we both got back to Calgary.

Avoid the Pitfalls

An 11 day can sometimes be stressful, but you choose your attitude. Your attitude dictates your experience at all times, but it is extremely important on an 11 day, and will help you to manifest and create either a positive or distressing situation.

You are vulnerable to discordant energy today. Avoid it by staying away from places where people may not be sending out high frequency vibrations, and by visualizing protective white light around you.

Your powers of manifestation are greater today, so be aware of the thoughts that you are holding and the vibrations that you are sending out.

Proactive Choices for Your 11 Day

Begin your day and all of its activities with a positive intention for yourself and others.

Set or review your priorities, and be willing to adjust your schedule. Be open to the interesting developments that can occur on an 11 day and the delightful rewards of a positive attitude.

Channel your energy and emotions in appropriate ways: consider the impact of your spoken and written words, and place your attention on what you truly want to bring into your life.

This is an excellent day to write in your journal, work on a vision board, and write or repeat positive affirmations.

The number 11 brings inspired creativity, and favours composing music or poetry, writing books and articles, and working on artistic projects.

Go to a movie, especially one that you are likely to find inspiring or thought provoking.

Because the 11 has a strong connection to electronic media, it is a great day to make recordings or videos, work on a website, host a webinar, or do anything related to the internet.

If you are in the market for new electronics, this is a good day to go looking. (Don't buy anything during a Mercury retrograde phase. This happens three times a year and it is not a good time to buy electronics.)

Just as you are sensitive to discordant energy, you are also highly receptive to positive, uplifting energy from pleasant interactions and nurturing environments. Intend to receive and integrate this energy for your highest good.

Have a Reiki treatment or see some other healing practitioner who can help you balance your energy. If you are a healer yourself, this is a good day for you to give treatments.

See a reputable psychic practitioner, attend a lecture, or find a way to connect with people who are on the same level intellectually and spiritually.

If you are a business owner, use your heightened profile today to talk to people and promote your products or services. Look into ways that you can get publicity for a current project or a new initiative.

If you have an 11 day while on vacation, choose your activities carefully. You're not likely in the mood for dealing with crowds. Depending where you are, this would be a good day to visit a beautifully restored mansion, or a spectacular scenic beach at sunset.

End your day with gratitude.

If Your Partner is Having an 11 Day:

Prioritize any information that you must share with your partner, and keep it as brief as possible. He needs facts today, but not in large doses.

Encourage him to step up efforts with regards to promoting his talents, products or services.

Be a good listener, as she may need to vent a little, or possibly share some new and exciting ideas.

Make sure she is able to get some time to work out, or at least suggest a walk together to help release any pent up nervous energy from the workday.

If Your Child is Having an 11 Day

Anyone having an 11 day may be on edge and children are no different. In fact quite often children are more intuitive and sensitive than adults.

Set a limit for time spent with electronic media. We should always be careful about how much television our children are watching and what kinds of programs they are being exposed to. Images of death and destruction through videos or computer games will always diminish your child's emotional health, and the impact is particularly strong on an 11 day.

This day will bring a good opportunity for you to role model and teach your child about healthy ways to find outlets for nervous energy. It is a great day to do some yoga together and to teach your child to calm down through breathing exercises.

Provide a calm atmosphere and start the process of getting ready for bed a little earlier tonight. Allow your child time to become accustomed to each shift of energy and activity through the day.

If You Are Single

If you are single and looking for a significant other, you are definitely going to be noticed today. The energy around you is magnetic, so get dressed up and go out to that social gathering!

Do some affirmations and visualization before you go out to further improve your chances of meeting someone and connecting in a positive way.

Notes About My 11 Personal Day

Your 22 Personal Day

The Nature of 22

Are you feeling on top of your game today? Are you feeling positive and energetic? Are there some little light bulbs going on…perhaps some unexpected "aha" moments, as answers to problems seem almost to flash before your eyes?

Today is your 22 day. Its element is water and its astrological body is the moon. Since 22 is the higher octave of the number 4, there will likely be important work for you to attend to. This day tends to move along at a balanced pace, as long as you don't overdo your commitments. At its finest, the master number 22 brings a powerful combination of inspiration, dedication, and motivation.

Healing and Empowerment

Jean has been dealing with arthritis and fibromyalgia for several years. She began a recent 22 day with a guided meditation which focused on empowerment.

This helped her to feel strong and she reported that her limbs "did not feel laden down like they sometimes do." She felt very present, and in the moment. She enjoyed several harmonious interactions at work, and felt that she had connected with others on a deeper level. Jean also went for a long and enjoyable walk by a river that flows through her neighbourhood, and felt truly inspired by her connection with nature. She wrote, "I made sure to thank Mother Earth for sustaining me and my loved ones."

There is a money theme that runs through a 22 vibration. It deals with earned money as a result of providing value for others. You may hear news about money, make a sale, or receive a cheque in the mail. I was amused recently to discover that the letters in the word "jackpot" combine to a 22. What a great day for feeling blessed and abundant!

This is a perfect day to be out in public, meeting new people and touching base with friends and acquaintances. If you are in business, it is highly likely that one of your customers will make a major purchase, or you will receive a booking from a client. If you are working for someone else, you may be given a new assignment, one that will really please you and could lead to further opportunities within your company. In addition to financial remuneration, the 22 day will also bring acknowledgement on the part of customers, co-workers, and employers for the quality of your work and contribution.

You are in the moment today. You feel alert, and you want results. It's possible that you may have an opportunity to get something done that's been on your mind for a long time. You will do it competently, and with efficiency; and you will achieve positive results. Even if it's one of those mundane house-keeping chores that can sometimes seem to bog you down, such as filing paperwork or paying bills, you seem to fly right through it on your 22 day, and have plenty of time for other important things as well. You might even wonder why you put it off for so long when it turned out so well, but that is because you were so intuitively "in the flow" with Divine Wisdom and Timing.

Before this day is over you may have the answer to a problem. The most logical course of action, the path of least resistance, may be so clearly obvious that you wonder why you hadn't seen it before. It may even come as a gift from the Universe. It may be something of major consequence for you, such as a job offer, or it may be as simple as finding just the right yarn for a knitting project, or just the right tree to plant in your back yard.

Another possibility on this day of strength is that someone you meet or already know may come forward to assist you in achieving the results you are looking for.

The 22 day brings a sense of being "in the flow." Even if it is mostly a day of relaxation, something important will be accomplished and you will feel that your time has been well spent.

Avoid the Pitfalls

There is a lot of physical, emotional, and mental energy running through you on a 22 day.

If this energy is not channelled wisely you may feel depressed, or have trouble sleeping at the end of the day.

Be careful not to deplete your physical and mental stamina by working too hard. Pay attention to how your body feels.

Avoid being moody. If you feel a sulk coming on, play some lively music, or better yet, take a half hour for some physical activity.

You will need some time in the evening to "wind down" from the day's activities before you go to bed.

Proactive Choices for Your 22 Day

Begin your day and all of its activities with a positive intention for yourself and others.

Get a good sleep the night before your 22 day and plan to apply focused effort throughout your day.

Write in your journal.

Make sure that you get out today. To make the best use of your 22 day you need to be interacting with others.

This energy favours any effort to improve your physical health and it can be especially helpful if there are issues around bones and muscles. Exercise, time spent in nature, (especially near water), good nutrition, will all be particularly well received and integrated on a 22 day. It's also a good day to see a medical practitioner.

Take on one of those daunting tasks that has seemed so overwhelming, especially if it involves organizing and taking care of finances. For example, spend some time organizing receipts for your taxes or looking for a file that has been missing for a while. Just set a limit to how much time you spend and don't get too bogged down in the details.

Review long term and short term goals. Work on something of major importance. Give a significant amount of your time today to a priority item.

This energy favours travel. It's a good day to book flights or even better, book a cruise. It's also a good day to organize your itinerary, travel and hotel confirmations, packing list etc. for an upcoming trip.

Your 22 energy helps others see and appreciate your talent. Use this day to submit resumes, go for a job interview, ask for a raise or apply for a promotion.

If you are dealing with troublesome issues as a parent, your 22 day lends its energy to any "tough love" situation that may arise. It's a good day to plan and prepare for a discussion with your child or teenager. The 22 energy will help you to get clear on your expectations and desired outcomes. Discussions held at this time could bring positive results, especially if your child is having one of his more receptive days, such as a 2 or a 6.

If you have to deal with difficult or adversarial situations, especially those that concern your finances, the odds are in your favour on a 22 day. It's also a good day to meet with your financial advisor for an investment review, and even to roll up those coins you have been saving and get them to a bank.

If you are a business owner, try to schedule important meetings on a 22 personal day. This energy is particularly powerful if you are dealing with large groups, international organizations, or charities.

If you are having a 22 day while on vacation, consider the best possible outcome for this trip. Is it meeting someone new, enjoying a new destination, replenishing and restoring your life force energy? Be consciously aware of your intentions as you fill your day with whatever activities appeal to you. You will most likely have a high level of strength and stamina today, so plan to do some activities that will make the best use of your physical energy. Spend time near water if possible.

End your day with gratitude.

If Your Partner is Having a 22 Day

Make sure that he has time for some physical activity, so that the energy flows and gets used wisely. Just as you do on a 4 day, suggest that your partner spend some time outside.

This master number favours laying firm foundations. It is a good day to discuss your finances and review long and short term plans for saving and investing money. If you have been hoping to move to another home, or to have one built, this is a great day to look at show homes together or check the on-line listings.

Be his best cheerleader today! It's entirely possible that your partner won't have a lot of time to share with you, but do be available to listen to plans, and encourage him to think about the big picture. Ask about the desired results, so that you can send your positive energy to the same project.

If Your Child is Having a 22 Day

Talk to your child early in the day about something that she would like to accomplish. As with the 8 day, help her to see the big picture.

Talk about steps that she can take toward attainment of short and long term goals.

Your child may be moody or irritable today so try to keep him away from sugar, food colouring, and other additives that are known to aggravate this situation.

Suggest playing outside or going for a run or a bike ride. If he is playing on a team, this would be a good day for you to make sure that you are at the game or available for at least part of the practice session.

If You Are Single

If you are a man, the energy of your 22 day will enhance your ability to connect with feminine energy. If you are a woman, your femininity, personal magnetism, and intuition will be strong today.

Similar to the 8 day, consider directing some of your energy toward a philanthropic cause, as in addition to that warm feeling that you get from helping others, you are likely to expand your network of acquaintances.

This would be a good day to go to the gym, or go hiking with a group of people who also enjoy outdoor activities.

Notes About My 22 Personal Day

Your 33 Personal Day

The Nature of 33

Do you have strong convictions today and a keen desire to make a difference?

Are you thinking of others and perhaps advocating for some marginalized group or finding ways to help victims of a natural disaster?

Well that's a lot to take on in one day; but you have high hopes and a sense of purpose. You understand your connection with your global family. You know that your positive intentions and affirmative action will have far reaching consequences.

This is your 33 day. Its element is fire, its planet is Mars, and its energy is both spiritual and emotional. Like the 6 and the 22, this is a day that often moves along at a balanced pace, as long as you don't take on too many commitments.

For Those in Need

Rhonda attended a prayer shawl meeting at her church on a 33 day. Her group makes shawls to give to people who are ill, or in crisis. They have given out over 200 shawls in the last three years. After working on it all summer, Rhonda finished her twelfth shawl that day and left it there. She wrote, "It feels so good to finish a project".

It is possible on a 33 day that your activities and concerns may revolve mainly around family and friends, just as they would on a 6 day. There may be a need for you to make a choice that puts your own current priorities or interests on the back burner in order to take care of someone who needs your assistance.

You may also be aware of an injustice that is unfolding or has taken place. Perhaps something is not right for you or a member of your family, and you have a strong urge to set the record straight. You will command attention today. Your values are abundantly clear, your opinion carries influence, and you are acting in integrity.

The creative energy of 3 will be elevated by the number 11 today. The Universe will connect you with an audience and you will feel strongly guided to share an important message with them. Your imagination soars and there may be opportunities for you to write, teach, sing, or perform on a stage. At the end of the day, you are likely to feel certain that you have made a meaningful contribution.

Avoid the Pitfalls

Be careful not to take on too much in terms of work or responsibility today.

Guard your energy levels and be sure to get enough rest the night before your 33 day. This will help you to avoid becoming moody or irritable.

Be sure to distinguish between what you can and can't change about your life or anyone else's life.

Be careful not to slip into a mindset of "righteous indignation". That particular type of thinking can diminish our energy and leave us operating on the wrong side of the Law of Attraction.

Be aware of the possibility that you may feel moody or prone to depression.

Make the Most of Your 33 Day

Begin your day and all of its activities with a positive intention for yourself and others.

Be ready to share your knowledge, wisdom, and talent with others. Teach a class or participate in a stage performance.

Write an important letter that will state your case and indicate your expectations with regards to any situation that needs to be resolved.

If you are hoping to gain support for a worthy cause or a position that you have taken, this is a good day to speak to friends and family members, or to place a phone call to some authority figure who you think can help you.

Do some volunteer work with a charitable organization.

If you are a business owner, this day favours leading a company training session or stepping up a marketing campaign. You might also like to join other business owners in support of a charitable cause such as a food bank drive.

If you are on vacation while having a 33 day, just as you do on a 9 day, find a way to connect with local people. For example, you may enjoy attending a concert that features local singers, dancers, and costumes.

End your day with gratitude.

If Your Partner is Having a 33 Day

This is a great day to be your partner's best cheerleader. If he's had a rewarding day, he'll appreciate an enthusiastic audience, and if there have been some tough decisions to make, he'll need you to be a good listener and to provide some fresh perspective.

If you are both able to enjoy an evening out, this would be a good night to go to a concert.

If Your Child is Having a 33 Day

This is a good day to enhance your child's self esteem and confidence, particularly in the area of visual or performing arts. Bring out the crayons or craft supplies and encourage your young one to create something.

It's also a good day to develop empathy and encourage your child to do something for others who are less fortunate.

If You Are Single

If you are single and looking for a significant other, it's possible that you're not thinking too much about your own personal circumstances today. You may indeed meet someone, simply by being out and about, but it's unlikely that this would be your objective. The double energy of 3 today makes it a good day to go out and see people, and seems to particularly favour activities with a musical theme, such as a dance or a concert.

Notes About My 33 Personal Day

Connecting With the Energy of Your Personal Day

You will not experience every aspect of your personal day number in one twenty-four hour period; however, as you review the descriptions for each day, you will notice that several elements of that number have come forward in your mindset, or your experiences and interactions throughout the day. Making notes over a period of two or three nine day cycles will bring you some amazing "aha" moments, and you will start to come up with some of your own great ideas for making use of your Personal Number System. You will see how working proactively with the energy of numbers is setting you up for positive results in all areas.

Don't work hard at this, just allow or release. Anything that's important will come to the surface.

How and where did you most notice the energy of your personal day?

Was there a particular event, theme, or situation that seemed to occupy your time and attention for a significant part of the day?

Did you notice a difference in your mood or your ability to focus?

How was your energy level or physical/mental/emotional stamina?

What kinds of interactions did you have?

What worked well for you today?

Did you feel particularly pleased with a certain accomplishment or outcome?

Were there any frustrations or areas of resistance?

Did you use your Personal Number System to plan anything for today?

How do you plan to use the energy of tomorrow's personal day?

Do What Must Be Done

Do not allow the numbers of your temporary vibrations to dictate your life. Simply make an effort to understand the energy that each number brings to your current reality, and whenever possible make the best use of that energy to assist you in achieving long and short term goals.

You must do what you need to do on any given day. Couples need to discuss problems when they arise. Children need to learn to be helpful or to do their homework all week long. Your family needs to eat every day, not just when your number 6 favours making delicious meals.

Compromise is necessary when you live with someone or when you are in the workplace. Sometimes there will be parties to attend on a 7 day, business meetings on a 9 day, travel to a distant location on a 6 day, or family members coming to visit on a 1 day, but most of the time these will not take up your entire day.

As you become more and more familiar with the energy of your personal day, as you become more conscious of how it is manifesting in your life at that particular point in time, as you set your intention to work with that number, to recognize, accept, and appreciate the gifts, the growth, and the opportunities it is bringing to you, as you mindfully and skilfully avoid the pitfalls and think in terms of the possibilities and potential, you will find that you are reaping the rewards of good timing, and that the Universe is moving you forward in a beautiful, well ordered progression. At the end of each day you will have a sense of fulfillment, achievement, and time well spent.

Your Birthday

Happy New Year! Your birthday is definitely a day to celebrate.

In addition to treating yourself or celebrating with family and friends, take some time to consider the significance of this day and what it means to you. Think about how far you've come, how much you've accomplished, and how much you've overcome. Acknowledge yourself and your parents, mentors, and role models who have been there to support you. You might enjoy making a donation to a favourite charity as part of your expression of gratitude.

On or just before my birthday I look back over the year and review some of the peak experiences that I have been able to co-create with Spirit in the past twelve months. I do this with great love and gratitude, reliving the joy of those special occasions and glorious moments, connecting with the good feelings, and intending to carry that positive, life enhancing energy with me into the future. My husband and I have birthdays two weeks apart, so we enjoy doing this together.

Of course, for all of us, there are days when the learning curve is not so gentle, and we feel as though our dreams are in danger of being permanently placed on the back burner. It's not fun to look back on those events, but it's definitely worthwhile to find the gift, reflect on the learning, declare them over and done, and release them.

Become familiar with the energy of your coming year and plan to make the best use of that energy to bring you closer to attainment of certain goals. Write out the features of your personal year that you find most appealing, and place them in a location where you will see them regularly.

Set some goals that are in alignment with your personal year. Consider all areas of your life, including work and productivity, finances, personal growth, professional development, contributions to loved ones, contributions to your community and global village, and personal enjoyment. For best results, your goals should be authentic, realistic, measurable, attainable, and focused on the actions more than the results. (For example, "I'm going to eat more fruits and vegetables and fewer carbohydrates", not "I'm going to lose weight,"; "I'm going to set up an automatic deposit into my savings account", not, "I'm going to save money".) They should be goals that feel right for you, not goals that you think you should set to please someone else.

The interesting thing about personal year goal setting is that many of the clients I meet, regardless of whether they know anything about numerology or not, are instinctively tuned in to the vibration of their year. For example, they are already thinking in terms of "getting organized" as they approach their 4 year, signing up for some courses in their 7 year, or running a marathon in their 8 year. Learning the number of their personal year validates their goals. They gain clarity, conviction, and a stronger sense of purpose.

I enjoy my birthday goal setting each year. I start to think about it several weeks before my Personal New Year (birthday), and often find that it takes a few days to complete the writing. It doesn't matter if it's not done in time for your birthday, as long as you are working on writing your goals and committed to completing this important process.

Studies have proven that written goals are more likely to be achieved, and that people who attach a date to the attainment of their goals tend to be the most successful of all in achieving them. After you have written your goals and eliminated any that do not resonate for you, rewrite them on a good piece of paper, with a date for each goal. Add your signature and if you wish, include an affirmation. You may actually wish to make two good copies. One can be folded and placed in a special spot in your home, with a crystal of your choice and perhaps a few other treasured items; and one can be placed where you will be able to see and read them on a regular basis.

If you like doing vision boards this can be a great time to get those creative juices flowing. If you enjoy writing rather than making a collage, consider writing a script or fictitious letter to someone, describing in detail the particular goal that you have attained, and the specific blessing that you have been able to co-create. (Vision boards and Law of Attraction journals are wonderful ways to celebrate your birthday, but of course you will want to put energy into working with the Law of Attraction at other times during your year as well.)

Find a crystal that will bring extra strength and enhance the experience of your upcoming personal year. Refer to the Numbers at a Glance section at the back of this book, or use your own intuition in choosing one that "speaks" to you.

Each number has a corresponding colour and element. Consider ways to bring that colour or element into your life this year. For example, I have a student who is an artist, a Native dancer, and an accomplished and creative seamstress. Each year she sews a new outfit for her dancing, and it is always in the colour that honours her personal year.

There may be small changes that you could make in your routines or thought patterns that would move you closer to your desired outcomes. Write some New Year's resolutions for this coming year. Think in terms of acquiring a healthy habit to replace something that is diminishing your mental, physical, emotional, or spiritual well-being. Just like goals, your resolutions must be realistic. These are promises that you are making to yourself, and you must feel that you are able to fulfill them.

Go for a psychic reading, astrology reading, or numerology personal year forecast. I am a numerologist with highly developed intuitive powers myself, but I love to go for a psychic reading. This is one of the few times when it is socially acceptable to spend an hour talking about yourself! A reputable reader will help you to gain perspective on your past and current experiences, and give you an understanding of how best to work with the energy that is coming up in the near future. (A reputable reader will not predict death or disaster.)

Spend quality time on an activity that brings joy and replenishes your life force energy. In other words indulge in something that leaves you thinking and saying "Life's GOOD!!" For example go for a lovely walk in a favourite park or natural setting, take yourself out to an art gallery or museum, go to a live theatre production, a concert or a sports event, spend an afternoon in a book store or walking around a favourite part of your town or city, enjoy a cappuccino or a scrumptious piece of cheesecake. However you choose to spend your birthday, do intend to honour yourself, and the significance of your day.

Be Your Own Best Friend

How would you like to spend your next birthday?

Make a list of treats and life-enhancing activities that would make your day special and memorable.

Part Five
Your Ongoing Success

Your Time is Your Life

How do we make each day count? How do we get what we want out of our time at work and at home? How do we get what we want out of life?

In your reflective moments consider what you can do and are doing to make each day count. Below you will find some suggestions that you can integrate with your Personal Number System to help make your life less stressful and more fulfilling.

Think of the Big Picture

Do you feel good about the way you spend your time? Be aware of the big picture of what you are doing, why you are doing it, and how the benefit of your actions ripples out to touch the world.

You might think that is easy if you are writing a book, or working for a charitable cause; but even activities that seem to be the most mundane or inconsequential ways to spend your time either contribute to or diminish the quality of life for all. We are all one.

Organizing your desk so that your work will flow more efficiently, taking a few moments to smile and say hello to a senior citizen, cleaning your house so that it is a pleasant place to live, growing a garden, or reading a story to a small child - all contribute to the overall well-being of humanity.

Plan Ahead

It is essential to make use of your calendar, your day book, or whatever electronic device you have. Write in everything you need and want to do, keep it up to date, and refer to it daily. Look up from what you are doing today to see what you need to do next week or next month. Look at the horizon.

Avoid Multi-tasking

Some people like to multi-task and the number 11 sometimes supports this habit; however, for the most part, it is not a practice that serves us well. Multi-tasking creates stress and adds pressure to our day. It fragments our energy and very often prevents us from completing tasks and projects on time and to our satisfaction.

Avoid Getting "Bogged Down"

From time to time we all have to take care of important but time consuming housekeeping tasks. I once went to a seminar for business owners. The facilitator suggested using a kitchen timer, especially when doing tedious but necessary tasks. Set an appropriate time limit for sorting through bulging file folders, answering e-mails, or rearranging a book shelf etc. That way you avoid getting caught up with chores that keep you from attending to priority items. When your timer goes, it's time to move on to another item on your agenda, and you can come back to your "housekeeping" another day.

Prioritize

Stop and ask yourself whether what you are doing right now is serving you or others, and if there is something else that you could be doing that would serve you and others better.

Several years ago, at a workshop based on the teachings of Stephen Covey, (author of The 7 Habits of Highly Effective People), I learned about the following time management quadrants.

According to this grid, everything you do falls into one of four categories:

1 Important and Urgent	2 Important and Not Urgent
3 Not Important and Urgent	4 Not Important and Not Urgent

Quadrant 1 is where we are when dealing with an emergency of some type, for example a malfunction of necessary equipment at home or work, or a medical situation.

Experts encourage us to spend most of our time in Quadrant 2. This is where we experience the least amount of stress, and the greatest sense of accomplishment; where we carry out our responsibilities, work our plans, and make progressive gains toward personal and professional goals. I believe that recreational activities also belong in this quadrant. We must never undervalue our leisure time. We are best able to stay in the second quadrant when we plan and prioritize.

Poor planning or lack of clarity may put you right into Quadrant 3, which is not going to serve your highest purpose. You can get drawn into this quadrant when you take on a crisis that someone else has created through their own poor planning or procrastination. Stay clear on your own goals and personal boundaries, and say yes only if it fits in with your vision for yourself and your life. If it's not "YES!" it's "NO", if it doesn't feel right, it's wrong.

The final quadrant is where you go when you are wasting time, getting sidetracked, losing touch with the big picture. Set your intentions and stay out of Quadrant 4.

Be Honest

Be honest with yourself and realistic in terms of what you can accomplish in any one day. Don't compare yourself to other people, or compare your accomplishments to other peoples' accomplishments. At the end of each day make a list of no more than five items that you must take care of the next day.

Acknowledge Yourself

Take time to review your day or week, to see how much you have achieved. Your "to-do" list will always continue to grow. It will be depressing and overwhelming unless you take time to look at what you have accomplished, and reward yourself appropriately for completing tasks and projects.

Take Care of Yourself

Take mini-breaks during your working day. Get up and stretch, look out the window, step outside for a breath of fresh air, or listen to a favourite piece of music. Pay attention to your body and what it is telling you. Is it time for a snack? A drink of water? A walk? A rest? A sweater?

Be Aware of Habits

Some habits, such as exercising, meditating, or writing in a journal can serve you well, but some can be self-sabotaging. Does your behaviour match your goal? Be aware of habits that do not serve you and end up compromising your health, productivity, and Peace of Mind. Don't "beat up" on yourself, just give some thought to what you can do that would serve you better. (At this writing my number one bad habit is working on the computer too late at night. I find that when I exercise self discipline and stay out of my office in the evening, I sleep much better.)

Watch Your Language

Be mindful of your thoughts and your language, particularly when describing your life and your day. Minimize stress and restore Peace of Mind by reframing situations. Something good will come out of every situation no matter what.

My friend Sharon Carne, (www.soundwellness.com) a teacher, author, and sound therapist, accomplishes a lot every day. She says that years ago she decided never to use the word "busy" to describe her day. Sharon's days are "full", which implies that just as there is a great deal for her to do, there is also an element of richness to each activity and experience.

Avoid the word "should". If you are reading a book or watching a movie that interests you, (renewal and recreation), enjoying a pleasant conversation with a friend, (strengthening your connection with the people you care about), or having a much needed nap, (replenishing Life Force Energy), why would you compromise your Peace of Mind, and diminish the value of your experience by saying something like, " I should be taking the car for an oil change", or "I should be wrapping Christmas presents"?

By working proactively with your Personal Number System, you will find that most of the time you are making positive choices each day. You are scheduling chores and activities at a time when the numeric energy supports you and leads to desired outcomes.

If you know you need to do something else, do it. Procrastination will just make your life more difficult and could create an avoidable crisis. If it's an everyday necessity like making dinner, plan ahead, have groceries in the house, (if possible, take care of that on your 4 or 6 day), schedule activities so that you'll have time to do it, or make arrangements with your partner/ older children to share the responsibility.

If it's one of those occasional requirements, such as a routine medical appointment, think ahead and plan time for it, preferably on a 4 or 9 day. If it's something you need to do for your employer or your business, consider the big picture and be grateful for the opportunity to contribute to the workforce while earning a living.

If it's something you're doing for yourself, or your partner/family, something for your personal enrichment and enjoyment, be sure you give it priority in your life. At the end of the day you will always be grateful for quality time with those you love. If an emergency crops up, there won't be any question of "should". You'll deal with it the best way you can. Using numerology in a proactive way minimizes stress, and there tends to be fewer emergencies to deal with.

Pre-Pave

Be aware of the powerful role that your thoughts and words play in co-creating all of your experiences. For everything that you do, hold positive expectations; and state those expectations to yourself clearly and emphatically, preferably out loud. Whether it's something simple like "This chocolate cake is going to be delicious", or something more impactful, like "This client is receiving lasting benefit from our time together," your results will be enhanced by giving voice to your expectations.

Elisabeth Fayt is a highly successful business woman, international speaker, and author who is passionate about helping others co-create positive experiences and interactions every day. She teaches a Law of Attraction technique called "pre-paving", which, in her own words is "consciously choosing how you want to look, live, and feel through every part of your day and every part of your life." [4] You can read more about this technique in Elisabeth's book "Paving It Forward, The Energy of Creating", available through her website, www.elisabethfayt.com

Hold Intention and Gratitude

For each of the personal day numbers I have recommended that readers begin their day with a positive intention for themselves and others. On any personal day almost anything you do, within the parameters of honesty and integrity can bring benefit to yourself and others, if you do it with Intention and Gratitude.

Never do anything by "default". That doesn't mean that you can't change your plans, or that it is wrong to do so, it just means that we should always be mindful of our purpose.

If I'm about to sit down with a cup of coffee and a book, I consider with gratitude how fortunate I am to have a comfortable chair and a good book, and intend for this period of time to bring me the benefits of relaxation. If I'm going for a walk in the woods I intend to reap the healing benefits of

---

4   Fayt, Elisabeth, Paving it Forward, The Energy of Creating, Spirit Seekers Publishing Inc., Calgary AB, 2008

my connection with Mother Earth while giving gratitude for the beauty that surrounds me. If I'm writing an article or a book, I intend for it to bring value, information, and encouragement to my readers, and give gratitude for the opportunity to exercise my creativity.

Be Flexible

Do not be attached to the outcomes. If after all your planning and effort, you do not achieve what you had set out to achieve, it is probably because the Universe has something better in mind for you. Trust in Universal timing and never question the rescheduling of planned events.

Observe Spiritual Practice

Whether you have an eclectic, "new-age" spirituality, or follow the teachings of the more traditional religious groups, observing some sort of spiritual practice on a regular basis will enhance your day to day life and help you to enjoy a greater sense of connection with your place in the Universe. Reading inspirational books, asking a blessing for your food, meditating, chanting, saying prayers, are all ways that you can strengthen you connection with Spirit, and at the same time, enhance your own sense of personal power.

Take Care of Base Camp

Earlier in this book I referred to a movie about climbers going to Mount Everest. The narrator was emphatic about the importance of Base Camp. Much careful thought and effort is expended in setting up Base Camp before anyone ever sets out to climb the mountain. That way the climbers can embark on their trek up the mountain with complete Peace of Mind that all needs will be met and any emergencies or disruptions to their plans will be handled in the best possible way.

I took that to heart and considered what base camp meant to me. For me it was my home and family unit. I knew that, as a single parent, it was up to me to make sure that my children had nutritious food in the house, clean clothes, a place to do homework, a Halloween costume, a Christmas stocking, a story at bed time, and a decent night's sleep, just as it was up to me to make sure that the bills were paid and the car was running well.

Numerology has always been a valuable tool for me in all areas of my life, and in those days it helped me to run my household more effectively and handle my responsibilities as a mother. By understanding and working with the energy of each day, month, and year, I was better able to take care of details at home. That allowed me to devote my full attention to work without worrying about matters that were never much of an issue if they were attended to, but could be cause for concern if they weren't.

Those were not easy years for us, and not every day ran smoothly, but knowing how to make the best use of numbers helped us to function at our best through the week and enjoy some time together on the weekend. Today my three adult children are my best friends, and I know that the experience we shared has given us warm memories and brought us close together.

Appendix 1 The Things We Do

Personal Month or Year

The following lists include many potentially life-enhancing endeavours along with the numbers of personal years or months that favour those endeavours. The numbers in bold font indicate the <u>most favourable</u> months and years for each. The numbers also indicate the most likely time for these particular themes and opportunities to arise; however, you must meet your needs and act on opportunities whenever they arise.

Career and Finances

Apply for a promotion: 1, 3, 4, **8, 11**, 22

Go into a business partnership: **2**, 6

Join new professional groups: 1, **5,** 8, 22

Make a major career change: **1, 5,** 8, 9, 11

Network for business: 3, **5,** 11

Promote products, and services: **3**, 5, **8, 11**

Reduce spending and pay down debts: 2, **4**, 6, **8**

Run for political office: **3, 8,** 11

Serve on a committee at work: **4**, 8

Share knowledge through books or articles: **3, 5**, 6

Travel for business: 3, 5, **8**, 22

Start a new business: **1**, 4

Start a home-based business: 1, 4, **6**

Take a course in electronic media or computer skills: 1, 7, **11**

Lifestyle

Build a house: 1, **4, 6**

Buy or sell real estate: 4, **6,** 8

Buy a new vehicle: 1, 5, **8**

Go on a cruise: 1, **2, 3,** 8, 9,

Renovate or decorate your home: 4, **6**

Research consumer reports on big ticket items: 4, **7**

Take care of major repairs to your home or vehicle: **4,** 6

Take a vacation: 3, **5,** 7, 8

Work on a landscaping or gardening project: 2, **4,** 6

Personal Care

Gather information to prepare for a major decision: 2, 4, **7**

Have surgery: 4, **6,** 9

Start a diet or fitness program: 1, **4, 5,** 8

Personal Growth

Engage in self guided spiritual and metaphysical studies: **7,** 9, 11

Go on a spiritual retreat: **7,** 9, 11

Go to school: 1, 6, **7**

Take up new hobbies or interests: 1, **5,** 11

Teach or mentor: 3, **6,** 7

Travel abroad: 3, **5,** 8, **22**

Volunteer with a charity organization: 4, 6, **9,** 22

Relationships

Adopt or become pregnant: 1, 3, 4, **5, 6**

Cultivate a new romantic relationship: **1,** 3, **5,** 6

Develop new friendships: 1, 3, **5**

Get married: 4, **6,** 8

Go for relationship counselling: 2, 4, **6**

Travel to visit family members: 3, **6**

Personal Day

The section below lists many different activities, along with the personal day numbers that favour those activities. The numbers in bold font indicate the best and most favourable days for those activities.

Personal

Attend a seminar for personal interest: 1, 3, **6**, **7**, 11

Attend a spiritual gathering or religious service: **7**, 9, 11

Begin a class or a research project: 1, 6, **7**, 11

Buy:

- ○ Clothing or other personal items: **1**

- ○ Expensive items such as furniture or appliances: 4, or **8**

- ○ Groceries: 4 or **6**

- ○ Real estate: 4, 6, **8**, or 22

Clean and organize personal space: **4**, 7, 9

Compete in a sporting event: 1 or **8**

Connect with nature: 2, **4**, 7, or 11

Deal with tough disciplinary situations at home and school: 4, **6**, 7, **8**, 33

Exercise: Most people will have their own favourite form of exercise and usually will pursue that form of exercise over others most of the time. However, should you be interested in applying the energy of the numbers to your fitness program, the following list will show what activities are enhanced by the number of your personal day:

- ○ Aerobic exercise: **1**

- ○ Swimming, water sports: **2**, 22

- ○ Gymnastics: **3**, 6, **33**

- ○ Weight lifting, working out at the gym, hiking: **4**

- Walking: 2, **4**

- Cycling: **5, 1**

- Team sports: 2, **4**

- Yoga, tai chi, walking meditation: 2, 4, **6, 7,** 11

- Competitive sports, running: **1,** 4, **8**

- Golf: 3, 4, **8,** 22

- Dancing: **3,** 6, **33**

- Climbing, or "extreme sports": 1, **8,** 11

Meet with:

- A hairdresser or aesthetician: **3,** 6, or **9**

- A lawyer: 4, 6, **8,** or **22**

- A medical professional or holistic practitioner: 6 or **9**

- A psychic reader, astrologer or numerologist: **7,** 9, or **11**

- A travel agent: 1, 5, 8, or **22**

Get married: **3** or **6**

> (This would <u>not</u> indicate your Marriage path; it would simply indicate the best personal day for you to host your friends and family, celebrate your marriage, and enjoy the role of being a Bride or Groom. The marriage path would be determined by the actual date according to the calendar, just as your life path is determined by your date of birth. Consult with a reputable numerologist to determine the best possible date for your wedding.)

Invest money: **8** or 22

Look after repairs or maintenance on your home or vehicle: **4** or 6

> (Single women especially should be careful that they avoid a 3, 5, or 9 day, when they may get talked into spending more than necessary.)

Move into a new home: **1,** 4, or 6

Review your investments with an advisor: 4, 7, or **8**

Start a vacation: **1** or 5 (Some of the very best trips I've been on have started on a 1 day and ended on a 9.)

Sign agreements, contracts, or financial papers: 1, 4, 6, **8**

Work on:

- An artistic project: 1, **3**, 6, 9, or 11

- A decorating project: **6**, 9, or 33

- A writing project: 1, **3**, **5**, 11

Professional

Go for a job interview: 4, **8, 22**

Announce new policies: 1, 6, **8,** or 33

Attend a work related seminar: 1, **7**

Audition for roles in theatre productions: 1, 3, **8**, 11

Begin a business trip: **1** or 8

Catch up on paper work: **4,** or 7

Host a webinar: 6, 8, 9, **11**

Initiate a project: **1**, 5, or 11

Look for a job: 1, **4, 8**

Promote a project: 1, **3,** 5, 8, or **11**

Record a CD: 3, 5, **11**

Resolve conflict and gain consensus: 2 or **6**

Participate in a debate: 1, **8**, 9, **22**

Socialize with colleagues and clients: **3,** 5, **8** or 22

Work on your website: 1, 3, **11**

Write a proposal for new client (or for a grant or big budget project) 3, **5**, 8, **11**

Submit a proposal for new clients: 3, 5, or **8**

Appendix 2 Numbers at a Glance

1 **Key Words:** Independence and New Beginnings
Energy: Mental/Physical
Element: Fire
Astrological Body: Sun
Colours: Red, Burgundy
Crystals: Ruby, Carnelian, Hematite

2 **Key Words:** Partnership and Intuition
Energy: Emotional/Intuitive
Element: Water
Astrological Body: Moon
Colours: Orange, Silver
Crystals: Moonstone, Aquamarine

3 **Key Words:** Creativity and Expression
Energy: Emotional/Mental
Element: Fire
Astrological Body: Jupiter
Colours: Yellow, Gold
Crystals: Citrine, Topaz

4 **Key Words:** Structure and Organization
Energy: Physical/Mental
Element: Earth
Astrological Body: Earth
Colours: Green, Brown
Crystals: Aventurine, Rose Quartz, Tiger Eye

5 **Key Words:** Adventure and Change
Energy: Physical/Mental/Emotional
Element: Air
Astrological Body: Mercury
Colours: Turquoise, Aqua, Magenta
Crystals: Turquoise, Clear Quartz

6 **Key Words:** Nurturing and Harmony
Energy: Emotional/Physical
Element: Earth
Astrological Body: Venus
Colours: Blue, Rose
Crystals: Sapphire, Emerald, Rose Quartz

7 **Key Words:** Spirituality and Solitude
Energy: Intuitive/Mental
Element: Water
Astrological Body: Neptune
Colours: Violet
Crystals: Amethyst, Moonstone

8 **Key Words:** Strength and Action
Energy: Mental/ Intuitive
Element: Earth
Astrological Body: Saturn
Colours: Magenta, Gold
Crystals: Diamond, Citrine, Clear Quartz

9 **Key Words:** Completion and Release
Energy: Intuitive/Emotional
Element: Fire
Astrological Body: Mars
Colours: White, Violet
Crystal: Opal

11 **Key Words: Illumination and Enlightenment**
Energy: Intuitive
Element: Fire
Astrological Body: Uranus
Colours: White, Silver
Crystals: Diamond, Amethyst, Clear Quartz

22 **Key Words: Purpose and Vision**
Energy: Intuitive/Physical
Element: Water
Astrological Body: Moon
Colours: Silver, Gold
Crystals: Aquamarine, Pearl

33 **Key Words: Courage and Integrity**
Energy: Intuitive/Emotional
Element: Fire
Astrological Body: Mars
Colours: Blue, Violet
Crystal: Lapis Lazuli

Bibliography

Bunker, Dusty: <u>Numerology, Astrology, and Dreams</u>, Whitford Press, 1987

Bunker, Dusty: <u>Numerology and Your Future</u>, Whitford Press, 1980

Carne, Sharon, <u>Listen From the Inside Out</u>, Mountain Rose Music; Calgary AB Canada, 2010

DeCoz, Hans, and Monte, Tom: <u>Numerology, Key to Your Inner Self</u>, The Berkley Publishing Group, (a division of Penguin Putnam Inc.), New York, 1994

Drayer, Ruth A: <u>Numerology: The Power in Numbers</u>, Square One Publishers, 2003

Ellinwood, Ellae: <u>The Everything Numerology Book</u>, Adams Media, 2003

Fayt, Elisabeth, <u>Paving it Forward, The Energy of Creating</u>, Spirit Seekers Publishing Inc., Calgary AB, 2008

Goodwin, Matthew Oliver: <u>Numerology the Complete Guide</u>, Career Press, Franklin Lakes NJ, 1981

Javane, Faith, and Bunker, Dusty: <u>Numerology and the Divine Triangle</u>, Whitford Press, 1979

Jordan, Juno: <u>The Romance in Your Name</u>, De Vorss and Company 1984

Lawrence, Shirley Blackwell: <u>Exploring Numerology, Life By the Numbers</u>, Career Press, 2003

Lawrence, Shirley Blackwell: <u>The Secret Science of Numerology</u>, Career Press, 2001

Millman, Dan: <u>The Life You Were Born to Live</u>, HJ Kramer(division of) New World Library,1993

Resources and Websites

French, Karen L; Gateway to the Heavens, ygb Publishing Limited, Buckinghamshire, England, 2008

Author Karen L French unravels the mysteries of sacred geometry; and clarifies the significance of patterns in our natural surroundings, and the relevance of numeric energy inherent in those patterns.

www.karenlfrench.com

Helliwell, Tanis; Take Your Soul to Work , Random House of Canada, 1999

Author Tanis Helliwell shows you practical ways to apply eternal truths to your work and your life, for greater balance and well-being, and better results in all areas of life.

www.iitransform.com

Richardson, Cheryl: Take Time for Your Life, Broadway Books, a division of Random House, New York, 1999

Author and coach Cheryl Richardson has written a valuable handbook for conscious living and for creating life as you want it to be. The following website will also take you to useful podcasts and radio shows.

www.cherylrichardson.com

For a series of inspiring You Tube videos about leadership and personal development, visit author Robin Sharma's website:

www.robinsharma.com

For a wealth of information regarding time management see

www.time-management-central.net

For more excellent articles about time management and personal development visit

www.sidsavara.com

Learn More About Numerology

Personal Clarity Readings

Vikki provides accurate, insightful, and uplifting private numerology sessions in person and by phone to clients in all parts of the world.

Discover the raw potential in your name and birth date, the strengths and talents that you have brought forward from previous lives, the pitfalls that you must be aware of, the nature of lessons and blessings that you will experience in the near future, and the direction your journey is likely to take over the next several years.

Learn how your numbers affect your career aspirations and relationships, how you can best connect with your higher self, and replenish your life force energy.

Empower your journey with valuable information and practical strategies that you can implement right away.

Your one hour session will be recorded and you will also receive a written core number profile. Book your session today. Visit www.gotyournumber.ca

Born To Thrive Weekend

The Born to Thrive Weekend is an uplifting, soul-touching creative experience that validates you and your journey, and connects you on all levels with the profound and ancient wisdom of numbers. Learn how numbers shed light on past and present circumstances and guide you in co-creating your future.

There is a vast amount of information encoded in your name and birth date. You will receive 75 pages of insightful, reader friendly resource material, and learn how to create a complete numerology profile. More importantly, you will learn how to apply this ancient and valuable information, how to work in harmony with your unique number profile, for Peace of Mind and Positive Results in all areas of your life.

To learn more and to register for the next Born To Thrive Weekend, follow the links on www.borntothriveweekend.com

Gifts and Gratitude
CONNECTING WITH THE ENERGY OF NUMBERS

Gifts and Gratitude -

Connecting With the Energy of Numbers

In 2008 Vikki was blessed to channel vivid imagery that would help listeners connect with and understand the impact of numbers on all areas of their lives. Originally used only at workshops, this thirty-six minute meditation has been professionally recorded as a result of numerous requests from students who have taken courses in Canada and Japan since the spring of 2008. The inspiring musical accompaniment has been provided by world renowned sound therapist Sharon Carne.

Numbers are powerful centres of energy that lead us to our highest level of integrity and personal fulfillment. They affect each of us every day of our lives and in every way. Regardless of which numbers are dominant in your personal numerology profile, you can open your mind and heart to the blessings of each of the numbers 1 to 9, and learn how to use their energy in positive, life-enhancing ways.

In this uplifting, soul-touching meditation, you are guided on a solitary journey of empowerment. You receive gifts that are yours to keep and strengths that you may call upon at any time. You connect with your Inner Self. You connect with your Greatness. You connect on all levels with the Energy and Spirit of Numbers. *Gifts and Gratitude-Connecting With the Energy of Numbers*, will be a unique and lasting gift for your friends, and a treasured addition to your own collection.

Gifts and Gratitude is AVAILABLE NOW worldwide, and can be purchased through www.gotyournumber.ca or www.soundwellness.com

179

CPSIA information can be obtained at www.ICGtesting.com
Printed in the USA
LVOW102211290413

331460LV00005B/19/P